HOLDING THE MAN

Adapted by
Tommy Murphy
from the book by
Timothy Conigrave

CURRENCY PRESS
The performing arts publisher

CURRENCY PLAYS

First published in 2006
by Currency Press
Gadigal Land, Suite 310, 46–56 Kippax Street, Surry Hills, NSW 2010, Australia
enquiries@currency.com.au
www.currency.com.au

This edition first published in 2024.

Typeset by Brighton Gray for Currency Press.
Printed by Fineline Print + Copy Services, Revesby, NSW.
Cover design by Design at the Bay for Currency Press. Cover art by Micka Agosta.

Currency Press acknowledges the Traditional Owners of the Country on which we live and work. We pay our respects to all Aboriginal and Torres Strait Islander Elders, past and present.

NATIONAL LIBRARY OF AUSTRALIA

A catalogue record for this book is available from the National Library of Australia

Contents

Introduction: 'Holding Tim and John' *vii*

HOLDING THE MAN 1

Jeanette Cronin as May Gert in the 2006 Griffin Theatre Company production. (Photo: Robert McFarlane)

Holding Tim and John

Timothy Conigrave's memoir *Holding the Man* is one of the great love stories.

It has a special place in the Australian psyche. It was published in February 1995, a few months after Conigrave's death on 18 October 1994—a month short of his thirty-fifth birthday. Since then, it's never been out of print. It won the 1995 Human Rights Award for Non-Fiction. It was listed as one of the 100 Favourite Australian Books by the Australian Society of Authors for its fortieth anniversary in 2003. In 2009, Penguin published it in its Popular Penguins orange stripe series—a sign of a classic—making it inexpensive and widely available. My guess is that it's one of the most 'passed on' of Australian books. I've handed over more copies than I can count.

In many ways, it's a simple book. It's written in disarmingly straightforward prose, without literary pretension, and might be read simply as a 'growing up in the 1970s' story. It's deliciously full of references to music, films and TV programs of the period. But its candour and portrayal of superhuman endurance make it unsurpassed as an account of the devastation caused by HIV/AIDS in Sydney during the eighties and nineties, and incomparable as an account of a complex, conflicted, yet somehow complete love.

Tommys Murphy's stage adaptation of *Holding the Man* is now a classic in its own right.

The play premiered at Griffin Theatre Company in November 2006, selling every ticket, and returned to the theatre in March 2007 for a seven-week season, the biggest selling in Griffin's history. With the public appetite still unsatisfied, the production kicked on to the Sydney Opera House in May and to Belvoir in September. Remarkably, within the space of less than a year the show had four major seasons in Sydney. But it didn't stop. It went to Brisbane Powerhouse and Melbourne Theatre Company in early 2008 before landing in London's West End for a three-month run in 2010.

It was a singular experience. Over that time, we received more letters and emails about the show than any other I've ever had anything to do with, anywhere. Long, handwritten letters. For a great many people, despite age, gender or sexual orientation, the story touched a well. For some, the theatre became a place of remembrance and reclaiming; for others, it was a place of wide-eyed discovery; for others still, it was a place to hold a loved one in a tender act of repair.

Other productions swiftly followed. There were outings in San Francisco in 2007 (leading to the first North American publication of the book), New Zealand in 2009, at the State Theatre Company of South Australia in 2011, and in Los Angeles in 2014. The play is now produced all over the place—in Italy (in Italian), in London and the USA (again) and in community theatres in small towns and large centres. As I write, it's heading to a new major production at Belvoir, seventeen years after the play was last seen there.

Tommy was also responsible for the screenplay for the much-loved 2015 feature film, which now streams widely, including on Netflix. So, for the decade between the creation of the stage and film versions, Tommy was the committed caretaker of Tim's story. At all times he has shown an open heart and enormous generosity, using his prodigious talents to amplify this great love story.

*

In April 2005, I sat with Tommy on a bench in Beare Park, just below my apartment in Sydney's Elizabeth Bay. We'd just finished an outstanding season at Griffin with Tommy's first play on a professional stage, *Strangers in Between*. I loved directing the play, and audiences loved what Tommy had to share. At twenty-five, he had freshly revealed himself as a playwright of maturity and uncommon capacities. As any good Artistic Director would, I sought to find something else for him. I asked whether he had read *Holding the Man* and whether he thought there might be a play in it. He said he'd heard of it, but not read it. The cover—a blurry photograph of two partially naked men—made him dismiss it, he said. He later revealed that he was secretly thinking: *I hope he's not going to ask ME to do that.* I was thinking: *Tommy has the sensitivity, sense of humour, aversion to sentimentality, and unguarded theatrical imagination necessary for a stage version.* I asked him to read it.

I had long wondered about a stage version. I first encountered the book in early 1994, when I was staying briefly in Nick Enright's home. Nick had been Tim Conigrave's acting teacher at NIDA, and they were now good friends. At that time, Nick was often visiting Tim in hospital, or at other places, working on drafts of chapters. Nick told me that Tim's health was failing, and that working on the book was probably keeping Tim alive. There was a need to work quickly.

I remember typed copies of draft chapters sitting on top of Nick's piano. I would read these loose A4 pages, intrigued by the accounts of growing up in Melbourne and life in Sydney theatre circles not many years past. I would be amused at Nick's furious corrections of Tim's punctuation. *IT'S = IT IS!*, the thick pencil would often scream.

Nick was not only one of our finest teachers, but of course also a very talented playwright. So here was a playwright helping to shape a memoir written by an actor. Theatre was in the book's bones. In the late nineties, a few years after the book had become so loved, Nick was keen to find a way to support both a film and stage version. But it never quite happened.

When Tommy read the book, he wrote me a very personal email describing at length the experience of reading it on a bus journey to his parents' home in Queanbeyan and getting to the final chapters with his head on his boyfriend's lap, sobbing. This chimed with how so many others had first experienced the book. He then described how reading Tim's life was like reading his own. Tommy had no experience of HIV/AIDS—which made some of the book a startling revelation—but Tim's travels through student theatre and NIDA and work at Griffin Theatre Company tuned with many of Tommy's experiences. Tommy felt a profound need to tell the story for another generation. He saw the value of distance. He was twenty years younger than Tim would have been, and felt a mission. He wanted to make the play, for Tim.

I commissioned him and scheduled an opening night eighteen months hence. Nothing like a deadline.

*

When we began to develop our approach, we asked a lot of basic questions. Why should this book be a play? What part of the story do we focus on? What does AIDS mean, onstage, twenty years after the Grim Reaper?

At the simplest level, we acknowledged the story's connection with Griffin Theatre Company. Tim Conigrave was involved with the company during the mid-1980s, most notably as instigator and writer of the part-verbatim *Soft Targets*—Australia's first full theatrical response to HIV/AIDS—which followed the first production of Michael Gow's *Away* in Griffin's 1986 season.

Theatre is everywhere in the book. Tim and John came together via a school production of *Romeo and Juliet*. They were torn apart when Tim left to train as an actor at NIDA. Tim discovered he was HIV positive while devising *Soft Targets* at Griffin. A staged reading of his play *Thieving Boy* at Belvoir became Tim's reason for admitting to his friends that he had developed AIDS. Tellingly, in early letters to his publisher Tim calls sections of the book 'scenes'.

This simple observation suggested a *way* to tell the story—playfully, performatively, through the very idea of theatre—but not necessarily *what* story.

We wanted the love story. Initially, we were interested in the question: *Why do we hurt the ones we love, and how do we answer that?* Tim hurt John many times during their fifteen years together, and John absorbed the hurt. In story terms, AIDS might be seen as a metaphor.

Penny Cook, a great friend of Tim's, voiced a description of the book in a Griffin creative development workshop in March 2006: 'It's an apology to John.' The love letter in the book is not restricted to the epilogue. Every page is addressed to John to say sorry for all the pain and thank you for all the love. Maybe that's why Tim wrote John so idealistically—John according to the Gospel of Tim—and himself so judgementally. The book is a final gift to John. The play makes a point of this. Throughout, there are many gifts, mostly from John to Tim, and throughout we see writings of all kinds: pencil-case graffiti, letters, newspapers, scripts, scrapbooks, and finally the book called *Holding the Man*. In a quiet way, we sense the story, the final gift, being written as we watch.

Even the title is a gift to John. The phrase 'holding the man' is not explained in the memoir. It most obviously suggests an embrace, but it also comes from John's sport. In Australian Rules Football, 'holding the man' is an offence that incurs a penalty; in John's case, a cruel and undeserved one.

Tommy was both systematic and sensitive in how he went about the task. Early on, he broke the book down into little story bits. That Excel spreadsheet is vast and full of speculation. He also contacted anyone he could find who appeared in the book, and in lengthy conversations sometimes found himself cast as counsellor or confessor. Others contacted him, offering photos or documents or anecdotes. He consulted with those who were, at the book's time, on the front line of the HIV/AIDS battles. An obvious but sometimes unfathomable fact became apparent: these people are real, they loved, and they suffered. Though we meet them in a book, they are not the stuff of fiction, but of life. Tommy held that responsibility close.

Tommy adjusted the raw material of the book to meet his theatrical needs, just as Tim adjusted the raw material of his life to meet his storytelling needs. Not everything happens in the book as it happened in life, and not everything in the play happens as it happens in the book. Characters have been omitted and others conflated. Most notably, Juliet in the play is a fusion of several characters in the book, and so has a name we've invented. Details from various episodes in the book have found their way into single scenes in the play. Sometimes, the chronology is a little different. Somehow, Tommy has managed to retain the full sweep of the book, and through some conjuring trick we don't see what's missing.

*

As we approached opening night in Sydney, Tommy and I visited the Conigrave home in Brighton, Melbourne. The family had been terrifically supportive leading up to the production, and we knew that Tim's mother and father were coming to opening night. The thought of meeting them for the first time in the foyer was just too silly. We wanted to introduce them to the experience in a more respectful way. They would, after all, not only be seeing *themselves* on stage, sometimes in scenes that never quite happened that way in either the book or in life, but they would also witness the death of John and be reminded of things we could not predict.

It was a magical Sunday afternoon. Tim's younger brother, Nicholas, met us at the family home, but he soon left us alone with Dick and Mary-Gert. I think we spent maybe four or five hours in their company over some lovely glasses of Riesling. Strangely, we both felt that we knew the house—the phone, on which Tim and John had so many furtive conversations, was still there; a photograph of Topolino, the Italian Mickey Mouse and an important talisman in Tim and John's relationship, was on the fridge; down the corridor, we imagined the sunroom into which Tim would sometimes sneak when John stayed over. Sitting in this living room, where so many important family discussions and arguments took place, was a moving melding of fact and memoir, of past and present.

Gert shared how she had read the book in one sitting late one night, in the chair where she now sat. She showed us photographs, and paintings Tim had made. She told us how over the years people wrote to them, simply looking up 'Conigrave' and 'Brighton' in the phone book, then popping a letter in the post, hoping for the best. She kept shoeboxes of these letters, testaments to the power of the book and to the impact her son's life has made on so many. I suspect these letters had a powerful healing effect over the years.

Dick was more circumspect, as men of that generation often are, and indeed he reminded me of my own father. Yet he was clearly proud of his son, and charmed us. He saw the play several times—an experience that must have been particularly challenging, since he told us that he had never read the book. Dick passed away in 2009. In The *Age* newspaper, in a moving gesture to marriage equality then still eight years away, the funeral notice read in part:

> Loved father of Timothy (dec), Anna and Nicholas.
> Loved father-in-law of John (dec), Anthony and Hilary.

When we left the Conigrave home, Tommy and I stood on a corner searching for a cab. From out of a shop floated Depeche Mode's 'Just Can't Get Enough'. This was an important song for Tim and John, and was Tim's funeral march in St Canice's Catholic Church in Elizabeth Bay, just around the corner from where I'd had that first conversation with Tommy. The song closed the first act of our production. Tommy and I looked at each other, said nothing, but our eyes welled. What were the odds?

Tim's mum and dad were great supporters, and came to several opening nights. At the first Griffin opening, Dick said to Tommy: 'This won't be closure. Here's a new beginning.' Mary-Gert shared with an actor: 'This play is a way for Tim to live on. If he were alive, he'd be staging this tonight.' Mary-Gert even made it to the London West End opening of the play, visited the set of the film and appeared as an extra in the wedding scene. She passed away in 2018.

Our only contact with the Caleo family had been a letter from Tim's sister, Anna Davison, as Tim's literary executor, letting the family know, as a matter of courtesy, that she had granted permission for a stage adaptation of her brother's book. There was no reply.

But at the very first preview, just as the applause was fading, a young man sitting behind me tapped me on the shoulder: 'Hello. I think you've all done a great job. I'm Anthony Caleo, John's baby brother.' I was dumbstruck, but eventually asked if he would like to meet the cast. For some hours that night, Anthony shared stories with us. Three days later, he posted on a blog that fielded one of many online discussions about the book and play:

> *Hello there everyone, I am John Caleo's baby brother Anthony. I just wanted to say thank you for all your kind words as this story truly represents one of the most beautiful depictions of love and devotion in the modern era.*
>
> *I went and saw Tommy Murphy's adaption of* Holding the Man *at the Griffin Theatre and to my great relief, it was the most amazing live theatre experience I had ever been fortunate enough to attend ... All of the fondest memories about John floated through my mind whilst I absorbed the play, trying to reconcile why the most beautiful people are always taken from us. Unfortunately, it was incredibly difficult to witness his death in the play as it was portrayed so wonderfully and sensitively ...*
>
> *I will miss John forever and I feel complete after seeing this work of art. I now have closure.*

In 2015, just as the film of *Holding the Man* was coming to screens, Lois Caleo, John's mother, gave an interview on ABC radio:

> *I haven't read the book, I haven't seen the play and I haven't seen the film. I know a lot of people might find that strange, but I couldn't ...*
>
> *After John died, I would say I had a hundred letters and cards from people all over the world about how some of them were in*

that situation themselves ... The letters were beautiful and so understanding, and saying how much it helped them cope with their situation: it was wonderful ...

To help people understand the world and that we're all not the same, we're all born different and that's God's way—I think that's wonderful. If it does that, that is terrific.

*

Tommy never met Tim, but they are now good friends. Tommy has somehow understood the ineffable magic of Tim's storytelling and made the play both completely faithful to Tim's memoir and yet wholly his own. Both works acknowledge the pain, but elevate the wonder, make the familiar strange and the strange familiar, and invite us to understand, without sentimentality, what love and survival can be. Both, I think, leave us wanting more of their candour and charm, their joy of living, and their wisdom. Both, I think, in their own ways, are achievements of the highest order.

David Berthold

David Berthold directed the original production of *Holding the Man*. He was Artistic Director of Griffin Theatre 2003–06, Artistic Director of Griffin and La Boite Theatre Company 2009–14, and Artistic Director of Brisbane Festival 2015–19. He is currently Artistic Director in Residence at NIDA.

Matt Zeremes as John and Guy Edmonds as Tim in the 2006 Griffin Theatre Company production. (Photo: Robert McFarlane)

Robin McLeavy as Phoebe and Guy Edmonds as Tim in the 2006 Griffin Theatre Company production. Photo: Robert McFarlane

Holding the Man was first produced by the Griffin Theatre Company at the SBW Stables Theatre, Sydney, on 9 November 2006, with the following cast:

TIM	Guy Edmonds
JOHN	Matt Zeremes
MARY-GERT, JULIET, RHYS, ROSE, A QUEEN, LOIS, HARRY, NIDA DIRECTOR, DOCTOR 2, GIA CARRIDES, YVES STENNING, SHRINK, VOICES, NIDA ACTOR	Jeanette Cronin
NEIL ARMSTRONG, SCARECROW, DICK, BOB, DERGE, QUEEN 2, WOODY, FRANCO, DOCTOR 1, PETER KINGSTON, NIDA ACTOR	Nicholas Eadie
PHOEBE, ERIC, BARTENDER, PHILIP, NIDA TEACHER, BEN FRANKLIN, VALERIE BADER, ANGEL NURSE, VOICES, NIDA ACTOR	Robin McLeavy
DAMIEN, MARIE, BISCUIT, LEE, DOOR BITCH, PETER, RICHARD, DAVID FIELD, NURSE 1, WAITER, DR SAM, FATHER WOOD, VOICES, NIDA ACTOR	Brett Stiller

Director, David Berthold
Designer, Brian Thomson
Costume Designer, Michael Agosta
Lighting Designer, Stephen Hawker
Composer and Sound Designer, Basil Hogios
Assistant Director, Nic Dorward

Matt Zeremes as John in the 2006 Griffin Theatre Company production. (Photo: Robert McFarlane)

CHARACTERS / ALLOCATION OF ROLES

Two play Tim and John. The remaining four play all the other characters. The meaningful doubling is set out below.

1. TIM.
2. JOHN, MISSION CONTROL (voice).
3. MARY-GERT (Tim's mother), JACKIE, RHYS, QUEEN ONE, LOIS (John's Mother), HARRY, NIDA DIRECTOR, DOCTOR TWO, ACTOR ONE, VOICES AND NIDA ACTOR.
4. NEIL ARMSTRONG (voice for puppet), SCARECROW, DICK (Tim's father), BOB (John's father), DERGE, QUEEN TWO, WOODY, FRANCO, DOCTOR ONE, THEATRE DIRECTOR AND NIDA ACTOR.
5. JULIET, ROSE, ERIC, BARTENDER, PHILIP (New Romantic), NIDA TEACHER, ACTOR THREE, DR. SHEPHERD, VOICES AND NIDA ACTOR
6. KEVIN, MARIE, BISCUIT, LEE, DOOR BITCH, PETER, RICHARD (AIDS patient; voice for puppet), ACTOR TWO, WAITER, VOICES AND NIDA ACTOR.

A NOTE ON THE STAGING

This play is written for six actors.

Admit the theatricality. The show needs to be free-flowing. Many of the shifts in character can be achieved with minor costume elements, often without leaving the stage.

The play also has three, related moments of puppetry.

Chookas.

Matt Zeremes as John and Guy Edmonds as Tim in the 2006 Griffin Theatre Company production. (Photo: Robert McFarlane)

ACT ONE

The ACTOR PLAYING TIM *enters.*

ACTOR PLAYING TIM: [*to the audience*] Let's begin.

A small puppet spaceman enters.

TIM: [*to the audience*] At the end of the sixties the world seemed very exciting for a nine-year-old. Things were changing at an incredible rate.

The lunar surface. NEIL ARMSTRONG *is in conversation with the familiar voices and beeps of* HOUSTON MISSION CONTROL.

School. *Meanwhile,* TIM, *nine years old, is sitting crossed-legged next to* KEVIN, *watching the TV*.

NEIL ARMSTRONG: Okay Houston, I'm on the porch.

HOUSTON MISSION CONTROL: Roger, Neil. And we're getting a picture on the TV.

NEIL ARMSTRONG: I'm at the foot of the ladder. Going to step off the LEM now. That's one small step for man, one giant leap for mankind.

KEVIN: Is it really there? Tim, are they up there now on the moon?

KEVIN *touches* TIM*'s leg.*

TIM: Yeah.

NEIL ARMSTRONG: And Kevin is touching my leg. Houston, do you copy?

HOUSTON MISSION CONTROL: Roger, Neil. We're checking that.

TIM: The teachers are crying. Why? They're crying.

KEVIN *puts his arm around* TIM.

HOUSTON MISSION CONTROL: We're getting a heart rate off the graph, Neil.

NEIL ARMSTRONG: Yeah. I know.

KEVIN *puts his lips to* TIM*'s cheek.*

TIM: Don't.

KEVIN: I wish you were a girl.

NEIL ARMSTRONG: Kind of stirring, a buzz coursing through me.

HOUSTON MISSION CONTROL: Roger, Neil. Just ride it out.

KEVIN: Tim …

TIM: Just try to pay attention, Kevin.

KEVIN: Maybe we shouldn't play poofters anymore.

TIM: [*aside*] My god. I'm a poofter.

Backstage at a shopping centre, an actor costumed as the SCARECROW *from* The Wizard of Oz *has entered.*

SCARECROW: Who are you? You're not supposed to be backstage.

TIM: I'm Tim.

SCARECROW: Who?

TIM: Tim Conigrave. I am a friend of Juliet's. She's in the floorshow with you.

SCARECROW: Oh, you're Tim.

TIM: Yes, why? What have you heard about me?

SCARECROW: Nothing. What did you think of the show?

TIM: It was really good. Must be terrifying in front of an audience.

SCARECROW: Yeah well, shopping centre show, it pays the bills. I'm not really … I mean a lot of my ideas weren't taken on board. Some. I went to NIDA.

TIM: What's that?

SCARECROW: Acting school. The national drama school. Haven't you heard of it?

TIM: No.

SCARECROW: It's pretty famous but I left after second year anyway because it can be limiting. Juliet says you think you might be gay.

TIM: What? She told you?

SCARECROW: I'm a bit of a role model for her and the others. I only wanted to say, mate, don't you think it's a bit early to make that decision? You're only fifteen, aren't you?

TIM: It's not really a decision.

SCARECROW: You've got your whole life ahead of you. Do you have doubts?

TIM: No. Maybe at the start. Now I have unrequited fantasies.

SCARECROW: Look, just don't close off your options. That's kind of a motto for me.

TIM: Okay.

SCARECROW: Okay.

Enter JULIET. *She is costumed as Dorothy from* The Wizard of Oz.

JULIET: [*to* SCARECROW] Sorry, Bruce. Sorry about 'If I Only had a Brain'.

SCARECROW: Yeah, it happens. I know that.

JULIET: Hi Tim.

SCARECROW: Anyone waiting for photos?

JULIET: Some.

SCARECROW *exits.*

TIM: You told the Scarecrow I'm gay.

JULIET: Oh look, I'm sick of this. I mean you say you're gay, I've said that's okay. Big deal. Aren't you going to say anything about my performance?

TIM: It was grouse. Really grouse.

JULIET: Thank you.

TIM: You made a lot of shoppers happy today.

JULIET: Y'know, they're doing Shakespeare at your school with my school and I was thinking … You should audition with me.

TIM: Me? Aw, I couldn't do that.

JULIET: We'd spend more time together. Can you help me get my zip undone?

TIM: Sure.

JULIET: You know how David Bowie is a bisexual.

TIM: Is he?

JULIET: Yeah. He likes men and women.

TIM: I don't have feelings about girls—but the guys at school? All the time. That guy John, I pointed out at the dance—

JULIET: He had his girlfriend.

TIM: So did I.

[*Then*] Sorry.

JULIET: Maybe you don't really know until you have sex with a girl.

TIM: I had sex.

JULIET: With who?

TIM: Kevin, a boy from primary school.

JULIET: You did it in primary school?

TIM: Not till upper primary. It started with a game we called 'Poofters'. Another time too, more recently, at the footy oval, near my house.

JULIET: What?

TIM: A man named Terry I met on a train.

JULIET: A man?

TIM: A boy. About eighteen. But, he had a boyfriend.

JULIET: He cheated?

TIM: They had an arrangement. Just as long as they didn't bring someone home.

JULIET: Oh my god.

TIM: I know. I wouldn't do that if I had a boyfriend.

JULIET: And did you just start talking on the train? How'd you know he was a gay?

TIM: Um. Well. We got talking about the bass player from The Little River Band. And Terry had a magazine with pictures of men kissing in it so it was pretty clear where we stood.

JULIET: I hope you weren't in danger, Tim.

TIM: No. Terry was nice. I liked that it felt dangerous a bit.

JULIET: No, you mustn't. People get abducted, Tim. You're moving too fast.

TIM: You think?

JULIET: You're just fifteen.

TIM: I can't help it.

JULIET: Can you unzip me a bit more? I can't reach it.

TIM: This guy John is really quiet and gentle but good at everything. He's shy but popular and he has beautiful eyes, dark brown with these eyelashes. He's captain of the under-sixteens.

JULIET: Well I don't think he'll be—

TIM: No I don't think he's gay. Like I'd know. I don't talk to John. I never have. Juliet, I cried driving home from the dance.

JULIET: Why?

TIM: Dunno. Supertramp came on the radio and I hid my face from Dad and I cried.

JULIET: Tim, talk to him.

TIM: Talk to him?

JULIET *gives* TIM *a friendly kiss and exits.*

Classroom. JOHN *is checking over his homework. Class is about to begin.*

TIM: Is this … Is someone sitting here?

JOHN: Nup.

TIM *sits next to* JOHN, *who is more interested in his workbook.*

TIM: Do the homework?

JOHN: Yep.

TIM: Me too. Difficult?

JOHN: Nup.

TIM: Geography sux.

JOHN: 'Salright.

TIM: Yeah. It's alright.

Silence.

I'm in a play with your brother. Seniors' Shakespeare.

JOHN: O-ye?

TIM: Yeah. *Romeo and Juliet. The Most Excellent and Lamentable Tragedy of Romeo and Juliet.*

JOHN: Boring?

TIM: No. It's a love story.

JOHN: Playin' Romeo?

TIM: The competition.

JOHN: Who?

TIM: Paris, the one Juliet leaves for Romeo.

JOHN: Poor Paris.

JOHN *pays more attention to his workbook.* TIM *tries to sneak a glance at* JOHN.

TIM: You're up for the APS Best and Fairest.

JOHN: Think I've ruined my chances. Argued with an umpire. Which team do you play for?

TIM: I just play soccer.

JOHN: A soccer choc.

TIM: Used to play firsts basketball. I'm Tim.

JOHN: John.

TIM: Yeah.

JOHN: Better pay attention.

JOHN*'s pencil case is in reach.* TIM *gives into the urge and scrawls across it.* JOHN *is confused by* TIM*'s graffiti.*

[*Reading*] 'U shall win'?

TIM: The Best and Fairest medal.

JOHN: It's a new pencil case.

TIM: Sorry.

JOHN: Nah, s'okay.

TIM: [*aside*] This went on for ages.

TIM *finds that* JOHN*'s pencil case is now covered in their graffiti.*

[*Reading the pencil case*]
'There's hope for the living and hope for the dead,
But there's no hope for John cos he's gone in the head.'
I wrote that. It was funny at the time.
'If it feels good and hurts no-one, do it!'
He loops his lower-case 'l's like we're meant to.
'John has asked me to stop writing on his pencil case, so I won't do it anymore. See, I've already stopped.'

JOHN: [*reclaiming his pencil case*] You idiot.

TIM: Hey, congrats, hey. On your trophy.

JOHN: Thanks.

TIM: I need to update your pencil case now. Not 'U shall win'.

TIM *scribbles out the word 'shall' on the pencil case.*

'U Win.'

JOHN: When's your play?

TIM: Thursday and Friday.

JOHN: You must be nervous.

TIM: Shitting myself.

JOHN: Poor Paris.

TIM: Are you coming?

JOHN: Don't know much about theatre.

TIM: I thought you'd be coming cos your brother's in it.

JOHN: Guess I should try. Thursday maybe.

Enter DICK *and* MARY-GERT, TIM*'s dad and mum, at* ***Xavier School hall*** *after the show.* TIM *cranes to see if* JOHN *has shown up.*

DICK: Here he is. Larry Olivier.

TIM: I forgot my lines.

DICK: Oh no, we wouldn't have noticed except for the prompt you got.
MARY-GERT: I don't think I did notice.
DICK: Yes, you said—
MARY-GERT: Oh no I was just caught up in the emotion of it all.
DICK: Yes. Really good.
MARY-GERT: Who are you looking for, Tim?
TIM: No-one.
MARY-GERT: Do you have to see a teacher before we get away?

Enter JULIET *and her mum* MARIE.

TIM: No.
JULIET: Hi Tim.
TIM: Hi Juliet.
JULIET: This is my mum, Marie.
TIM: Pleased to meet you. These are my parents, Mary-Gert and Dick.
DICK: You must be very proud of your daughter.
MARIE: Yes. Lovely.
DICK: Few shaky flowers at the crypt.
MARY-GERT: Dick.
DICK: But very good.
MARY-GERT: [*to* MARIE] Weren't they lovely? Pleased to meet you.
JULIET: [*to* TIM] D'you sign my program?

As the parents talk, TIM *and* JULIET *have their own separate conversation.*

MARIE: [*to* MARY-GERT *and* DICK] Lovely, yes.
TIM: [*to* JULIET] Yeah.
DICK: [*to* MARIE] Yes.
JULIET: [*to* TIM] Did he come?
MARY-GERT: [*to* MARIE] The costumes—
TIM: [*to* JULIET] It was John I was imagining dead—
MARIE: [*to* MARY-GERT *and* DICK] Lovely.
TIM: [*to* JULIET] … at the graveside—
MARY-GERT: [*to* MARIE] Yes.
TIM: [*to* JULIET] … to make me cry on stage—
MARIE: [*to* MARY-GERT *and* DICK] Yes.
TIM: [*to* JULIET] … and he couldn't even bother to show.
MARY-GERT: [*to* MARIE] All the emotions, I thought. It had all the emotions.

JULIET: [*to* TIM] Maybe he'll come tomorrow.

MARIE: [*to* MARY-GERT *and* DICK] Lovely, yes.

JULIET: [*to* TIM] It'll be better then.

DICK: [*to* MARIE] Yes it was very well done.

TIM: [*to* JULIET] Yeah.

MARY-GERT: [*to* MARIE] Yes.

JULIET: [*to* TIM] I want to do plays forever.

MARIE: [*to* MARY-GERT *and* DICK] Lovely.

JULIET: [*to* TIM] We could have a dinner.

MARY-GERT: [*to* MARIE] Yes.

TIM: [*to* JULIET] Have to be girls there.

MARIE: [*to* MARY-GERT *and* DICK] It's important, I think.

JULIET: [*to* TIM] I'll bring a friend.

MARY-GERT: [*to* MARIE] Oh yes, terribly.

JULIET: [*to* TIM] Your place—

MARY-GERT: [*to* MARIE] Good socially, too.

JULIET: [*to* TIM] … Wednesday night—

MARIE: [*to* MARY-GERT *and* DICK] Yes lovely for them.

JULIET: [*to* TIM] … I'm cooking.

MARY-GERT: [*to* MARIE] Yes.

JULIET: [*to* TIM] Invite John.

DICK: [*to* TIM] Well, we should get going, you've got school tomorrow, son.

TIM: [*to* JULIET] You're so pushy.

MARY-GERT: [*to* MARIE] They work them hard.

JULIET: [*to* TIM] It'll work out.

MARIE: [*to* MARY-GERT *and* DICK] Work them very hard, yes.

MARY-GERT: [*to* MARIE] Lovely to meet you.

MARIE: [*to* MARY-GERT *and* DICK] Yes, you too, yes.

DICK: [*to* MARIE] See you then.

MARIE: [*to* MARY-GERT *and* DICK] Lovely, yes.

As JULIET *and* MARIE *exit:*

MARY-GERT: Well she was lovely.

DICK: Juliet's a pretty girl, Tim.

MARY-GERT: Very good actress, I thought. All the emotions.

Locker room. BISCUIT *and* JOHN *are getting changed.*

JOHN: Hi.

TIM: Oh. Hi John.

JOHN: Sorry I wasn't there on Friday. How did it go?

TIM: It went okay. Good actually.

BISCUIT: Err, bumchums.

TIM: Shut up, Biscuit.

JOHN: I was out on a run and when I got back there was this note from Mum saying that she and Dad had gone to Paul's play.

BISCUIT: Yeah, *Homeo and Poofter-ette*.

JOHN: That's when I remembered. Sorry.

BISCUIT: I thought you were boyfriends with me, Conigrave.

TIM: Sorry, Biscuit, my heart belongs to John.

BISCUIT: That's cool. We'll make it a triangle.

JOHN: I'll see you at the break.

TIM: And John, I'm having an end-of-term dinner on Wednesday night with some of the girls from the play. D'you wanna come?

BISCUIT: Don't play favourites, Conigrave.

JOHN: [*to* TIM] Getting home might be a bit difficult.

TIM: [*to* JOHN] Juliet lives over your way. I'm sure you could get a lift with her.

JOHN: Sounds good.

BISCUIT: [*to* TIM] We'll talk about this in bed, pumpkin.
[*To* JOHN *as they leave*] I'm good at being a gay hey.

JOHN *and* BISCUIT *exit.*

TIM: [*aside*] John Caleo at my place for dinner and—Fuck. Maybe you're only coming to meet some girls. Fuck.

TIM*'s place. Time leaps;* JULIET *and* JACKIE *whoosh in.*

JULIET: We wanted to get here before lover-boy.

TIM: Fuck.

JACKIE: It's alright, darling; I knew from the moment I met you.

Fuck, the doorbell!

TIM: [*aside*] Fuck. Doorbell—a bolt of lightning—your silhouette through the glass—schoolbag over your shoulder—dressed quite formally.

JOHN: I got lost on the way from the station.

TIM: [*aside*] Introductions.

[*To* JOHN] Jackie played Lady Montague. Juliet played Juliet. I played Paris.

[*Aside*] Silence—the girls stare.

Glasses of drinks have been distributed in an instant.

JULIET: You and Tim are at school together?

TIM: [*aside*] Disbelief at an obvious question—silence again—You fumble with your glass.

JACKIE: What did you think of the play?

JOHN: I didn't see it.

JACKIE: We were fabulous.

TIM: [*aside*] Silence—fuck—food comes out.

JULIET: [*delegating spots*] Lady Montague and me there. John next to Tim here. Dig in.

Whoosh, enter MARY-GERT.

MARY-GERT: It's only me. Won't disturb you. Promised to hide. Oh! That's an interesting seating arrangement.

TIM: [*aside*] More introductions—my mum—agonising crap—she wants to say something unimaginably embarrassing—

MARY-GERT: Such ruddy cheeks still.

TIM: [*aside*] Try—

MARY-GERT: Didn't notice he got a prompt.

TIM: [*aside*] She might as well say—

MARY-GERT: I once made the terrible mistake of serving asparagus hors d'oeuvres at a piss party.

TIM: [*aside*] Mum ushered away.

MARY-GERT *has gone.*

JULIET: We're a new group of friends, so we should pass a kiss around the table as a kind of bond.

TIM: [*aside*] Terror fuck—a plan afoot—I'm next to you—you'll refuse—Jackie and Juliet kiss—linger—wish I was a girl—Juliet up for air, then …

Silence for the first time in the scene as JULIET *and* TIM *kiss.* TIM *slams his hand onto* JOHN*'s leg.* JOHN *moves his hand onto* TIM*'s.* TIM*'s eyes light up.* TIM *turns as* JOHN *shuts his eyes and* *purses his lips. They kiss.* TIM *breaks free as* JOHN *opens his eyes. They catch sight of each other. We hear a snapshot of the girls' applause as time leaps again.*

JULIET: Bravo.

JACKIE: Sweet. Last but not least.

Wham, JACKIE *throws her arms around* JOHN *and gives him a smacker on the cheek. Fuck, there's that alarming fuckin' doorbell again.*

TIM: [*aside*] Doorbell before long enough.

Whoosh, enter MARIE.

Marie, Juliet's mum, is a taxi home.

MARIE: Lovely, yes, sophisticated, lovely, all very lovely—well then.

MARIE *jingles her keys.*

TIM: [*to* JOHN] Glad you could come and um, I'll see you at school tomorrow.

JOHN: Sure.

TIM: Cool. Yeah, um— [*a quick peck on the cheek*] goodbye.

JOHN: Bye.

Suddenly all but TIM *and* JULIET *have gone.*

JULIET: He's divine.

TIM: Do you think he's gay?

JULIET: It doesn't matter. He obviously likes you and that's all that's important.

Exit JULIET.

TIM: [*aside*] There goes the boy I've kissed. Marie, his life is in your hands. I better not hear you've had a head-on with a tram.

Caleo home. *Enter* BOB CALEO. *A phone is ringing.*

Conigrave home. TIM *is making a phone call.*

BOB: Hello?

TIM: Hello Mr Caleo, may I speak to John please?

BOB: Whom may I say's calling?

TIM: Tim. Tim from school.

BOB: John! Phone.

Enter JOHN.

[*To* JOHN] Mate from school. [*To* TIM] 'Tim'?

TIM: [*to* BOB] Tim.

BOB: [*to* JOHN] Tim.

JOHN: [*to* BOB] Tim? Oh?

As BOB *exits:*

[*To* TIM] Hi Tim.

TIM: Oh hi, it's Tim.

JOHN: Nice surprise.

TIM: Good. Um. There's something I want to tell you.

JOHN: I'm all ears.

TIM: I … Um … Well … What I'm trying to say is … John … I like you.

Silence.

JOHN: That's good.

TIM: I … I'm being serious. I like you. I really like you. I've liked you for some time.

JOHN: I like you too.

TIM: Does this mean we're going out together?

JOHN: You haven't asked me yet.

TIM: John Caleo, will you go round with me?

JOHN: Yep.

TIM: Oh.

Silence.

Have you ever had a girlfriend?

JOHN: One.

TIM: I think I knew I was gay when I was nine. When they landed on the moon.

JOHN: I don't know if I do know if I am.

TIM: Oh that's okay. Bi is better. Bowie is bisexual. Do you like Bowie?

JOHN: Mmmh. I've always wanted to be married with kids. I want kids.

TIM: I'll have to be their godfather.

MARY-GERT *pokes in her head.*

MARY-GERT: Tim please, you've been on the phone for ages, please.

TIM: Yep, Mum. [*To* JOHN] How do you, how do you reckon your family and stuff would react?

JOHN: Mmmh, not good.

TIM: No.

JOHN: Yep. And whatever happens, however things turn out, we'll always be friends. Let's agree to that.

TIM: Yeah, let's.

MARY-GERT *leans in.*

MARY-GERT: Please, Timothy. You have been on the phone for two hours. Please. Truly.

TIM: Okay, okay. [*To* JOHN] Did you hear that?

JOHN: Has it really been two hours?

TIM: Better go.

JOHN: I'll see you tomorrow.

TIM: Sleep well.

JOHN: You too.

TIM: I don't want to hang up.

JOHN: Me neither.

TIM: This is it, I'm hanging up.

JOHN: You didn't hang up.

TIM: Nup. Sweet dreams, my boyfriend.

JOHN: Goodnight.

Somewhere secret. *They pash.*

TIM: I can't believe this.

JOHN: What?

TIM: This. I've liked you for so long and now I'm here with you.

They kiss again. TIM *tries to reach into* JOHN*'s pants.*

JOHN: Better not.

TIM: Sorry.

JOHN: Better get home.

TIM: Sure.

JOHN: Better go.

TIM: Yep.

But they kiss instead.

No-one can see.

JOHN: My parents will be wondering where I am.

TIM: Okay.

JOHN: I wish we could hold hands in public.

TIM: Maybe one day. When things change.

JOHN: Yeah. Maybe. I really should go.

TIM: God, I'm so turned on, I'll have to go straight home and pull myself.

JOHN: You don't do that, do you?

TIM: Are you joking?

JOHN: Why do you need to?

TIM: Because it's fun.

JOHN: Y'know it's not good for you.

TIM: Says who?!

JOHN: Can you see if you can stop?

TIM: Yes.

[*Aside*] I lasted a day. Sorry, John.

BISCUIT *reads from a copy of* Sursum Corda, *the school magazine.*

BISCUIT: *Sursum Corda*: Xavier College Students' Magazine. Profiles of New College Prefects. 'Name: Caleo, John. Best friend: Tim. Highest accolade: 1976 Best and Fairest. Hobbies: Anything that involves Tim. Favourite colour: Essendon black and red or anything Tim is wearing.'

BISCUIT *exits as* JOHN *approaches* TIM ***at school.***

JOHN: Did you read *Sursum Corda*?

TIM: I saw. I don't care. I only wanted prefect so I could turn it down—to make a stand.

JOHN: My profile. They know.

TIM: Oh that? Doesn't matter.

JOHN: Walks a thin line, Tim.

TIM: It's not malicious, John. In a way it's kind of accepting. I spoke to Father Lewis about it and—

JOHN: What do you mean?

TIM: He reckons the staffroom gossip's been about you and me all year.

JOHN: You spoke to Father Lewis about us?

TIM: He worked it out. All the jacks did. He reckons whatever we do we'll do in dignity.

JOHN: Jesus. Why hasn't someone tried to stop us?

TIM: Lay staff want to, but the Jesuits look out for us. Seen it all the time.

JOHN: Oh my god.

TIM: It's alright, John.

JOHN: It's not.

TIM: Lewis says only magical people get talked about. I'm not in the student magazine, John. I'm mentioned in your profile, but not the *chosen twelve*.

JOHN: No. Are you okay you missed out?

TIM: Course, I am, yeah. Doesn't matter. I think it's revolting to set one group of boys apart, give them power and ask them to dob on their mates. It's just a form of policing.

JOHN: Not everything has to be political.

TIM: And they always choose the guys who excel at sport. I find the whole thing elitist.

JOHN: And?

TIM: And congratulations. The coffee scrolls are on me at lunch. I can't believe I didn't get prefect, y' bastard.

JOHN: Good.

TIM: You know, we could get Father Lewis to talk to our parents.

JOHN: About us? No way.

TIM: Well, if you don't think—

JOHN: Never. They can never find out about us.

TIM: Okay. Geography?

JOHN: We have a prefects' meeting.

TIM: Oh.

JOHN *exits ...*

... as DERGE, TIM, ERIC, RHYS *and* BISCUIT *bounce on in sleeping bags.*

A slumber party.

BISCUIT: I fucked the English exam. I answered all three fuckin' questions. Meant to select two. I've fucked Comprehension.

TIM: You knew to choose two.

RHYS: That was in all the fuckin' trials.

BISCUIT: That's what I'm fuckin' saying. I fucked it. I fucked it up the arse.

DERGE: Fuck it.

BISCUIT: I know. Fuck it. I don't care. What's fuckin' done's fuckin' done.

TIM: Fucking exams. Hate waiting for fucking results.

BISCUIT: Shut up, Conigrave. All school I've hated you fucks saying you're scared of a fuckin' result, you're smart, fuck off.

ERIC: Fuckin' hell. School's fuckin' done now.

TIM: You heard about the talent scout?

RHYS: What?

TIM: John's been selected by the Essendon under-nineteens.

BISCUIT: Fuck.

ERIC: That's great.

DERGE: Fuckin' deserves it too.

TIM: That's why he couldn't come up here. He's going to a training camp.

RHYS: Listen to you. Like his fuckin' wife. Or mum. Like his fuckin' mum.

TIM: [*as* LOIS CALEO] Well, I'm proud's all.

BISCUIT: Might mean he'll play for Essendon one day.

TIM: He will.

DERGE: Your mum and dad's fuck ranch is really nice, Eric.

ERIC: Fuck off.

RHYS: Thanks for having us up here.

ERIC: That's alright. Don't call it a fuck ranch please. I've been coming here since I was two. It's our fuckin' holiday house.

RHYS: They would fuck here a lot.

ERIC: Shut up, please.

DERGE: Hey, what's the most bizarre sexual thing you've heard of?

RHYS: Um, farm boys get the poddy calves to suck them off.

BISCUIT: Well, a Wesley guy cut the mut [*rhymes with 'put'*] out of a porno poster and put mince meat behind it and shoved it in a bar heater to keep it warm—

DERGE: That was you, Biscuit.

BISCUIT: Bull fuck. Piss off.

TIM: How do you all wank?

BISCUIT: Ease up.

ERIC: Backhand.

DERGE: What?

TIM: We all do it. I sort of pump the bed like I'm fucking it.

BISCUIT: Yeah well that's kind of what I do. Leave my jocks on and then put a flannel down the front and pump it.

RHYS: Don't you share your bedroom with your brothers?

BISCUIT: I can cum without making a noise.

TIM: I can cum quietly. I've cum at slumber parties with you guys before.

DERGE: Fuck off.

TIM: I've cum at camps and retreats and shit. I've probably cum with you lot in the room a thousand times.

ERIC: Yeah me too.

DERGE: Sometimes.

ERIC: I rub the head of my cock, that's my favourite way.

RHYS: Sometimes I do it nasty-fast like I'm feeding really hungry chooks.

ERIC: Yeah. I think I might do it now.

One by one, they start wanking in their sleeping bags. After some time ...

TIM: Um. So this is weird.

DERGE: Shhh.

Quiet batting.

ERIC: We should race to see who can cum first.

TIM: You're just saying that cos your way's so efficient.

ERIC: Yep.

Quiet batting.

BISCUIT: I have wanked three times a night since I was fourteen no matter where I was.

TIM: Still two more to go tonight.

BISCUIT: Just one. Did it before in the toilet.

ERIC: [*while wanking*] Better fuckin' of fuckin' cleaned it up, filthy fuckin' mongrel.

DERGE: Shhh. I'm concentrating.

Quiet batting.

TIM: I thought about cumming so now I'm going to cum.

ERIC: Oh. Me too.

ERIC *and* TIM *cum.*

DERGE: S'pose I better too.
TIM: Looks like the world's ending when Derge goes.
DERGE: Don't watch. Don't.

DERGE *cums with quiet, quick intensity.*

Man, far out.

And here comes RHYS.

RHYS: No. Nup. Na. No. Oh. Fuckin' dirty slut.

RHYS *cums and is suddenly silenced by shame. He shelters from the stares.* BISCUIT *is still wanking, buried in his sleeping bag.*

DERGE: A good stress release.
TIM: I wanked so much during study break.
ERIC: Oh red raw.
DERGE: C'mon, Biscuit, you can do it.
BISCUIT: Shut up.
ERIC: I hated not seeing anyone during study break. That was the worst thing about exams.
TIM: My worst thing … I was studying, one night, late, real late and my dad walks in and he puts his arm around me and he cries.
ERIC: When you're ready, Biscuit.
BISCUIT: Shut the fuck up, will you?
DERGE: What do you mean, Tim?
TIM: He cried.
DERGE: Why?
BISCUIT: Okay, I'm, fuck, I'm, fuck …

BISCUIT *roars!*

TIM: Quietly, hey?
ERIC: Your brothers must be deaf.
DERGE: Tim, how come your dad cried?
TIM: I dunno. He doesn't accept me.
BISCUIT: [*finally resurfacing*] What's to accept?
TIM: Thanks Biscuit. Circle-jerk buddies accept each other.
RHYS: Dead-set, we are not circle-jerk buddies.
ERIC: Yeah.

TIM: John and I are.

Silence.

John and I are lovers.

Silence.

BISCUIT: Youse two?

ERIC: What?

BISCUIT: I knew it. I knew it.

TIM: Did you?

BISCUIT: Fuck I fuckin' knew that.

ERIC: I didn't. Never thought …

TIM: Are you okay with it?

Silence.

ERIC: I think it's … because it's you and John, I mean, who are, who are you-knows.

TIM: That's why my dad cried.

RHYS: You told them? Why would you do that?

TIM: I was spending so much time with John and they asked why.

DERGE: What'd they say?

TIM: Dad said I'd grow out of it because boys do sexual things with each other sometimes—

ERIC: We don't.

TIM: And Mum said if I don't grow out of it, I'll have a sad and very lonely life. I got Father Lewis to talk to them.

BISCUIT: Lewis?

ERIC: Oh he's not one is he?

TIM: No. Maybe. He told Mum to make some new house rules and now John sleeps in the sunroom and we wait for them to be asleep before he sneaks into my room.

RHYS: And they're okay now?

TIM: I thought so until Dad goes 'please don't do this to us' and dripped tears all over my homework.

DERGE: What'd you do?

TIM: Nothing. I just sat there and rubbed his arm. What could I do? I've never seen my dad cry. And he kind of wiped his tears and said sorry and went out.

DERGE: Well, the circle-jerk brothers don't mind. You and John. We don't care.

BISCUIT: Yeah. You and John.

ERIC: Yep.

TIM: Thanks, boys.

Conigrave home. *DICK and MARY-GERT are waiting up. A cask of riesling is handy.*

DICK: Could you come in here, son?

TIM: Just a minute, Dad.

MARY-GERT tops up her glass of wine.

DICK: Can we see you please?

TIM approaches his parents.

TIM: Yeah?

DICK: You and John can't see each other anymore.

TIM: Yes we can.

DICK: His father was in my office this morning, waving a pack of letters at me and yelling that you had corrupted his son, a good Catholic boy, trying to make him homosexual.

TIM: Where the hell did he get our letters?

MARY-GERT: While John was staying here last night Mr Caleo went through his room. He obviously expected to find something. He accused your father of being a party to the whole thing.

TIM: He has no right to go through John's stuff.

DICK: Don't you understand? You're not to see each other. The man's threatening court action.

MARY-GERT: Who knows what he'll do next time?

TIM: And do you support him?

DICK: You listen, Tim. You know we've never been happy with this lifestyle you've chosen. We've tried to stay out of it, but this morning was the most humiliating moment of my life. You hear?

TIM: We're adults now. We're at uni.

DICK: Living under our roof.

TIM: You can't stop us.

MARY-GERT: Of course we can't. We can't stop you, Tim. But John won't be staying here anymore and you won't be invited to the Caleos'.

DICK: And you can't use the phone to contact him.

TIM: [*aside*] Sometimes you smash doors and furniture. But sometimes you grit your teeth and say with quiet disgust …

[*To* MARY-GERT *and* DICK] Fuckin' poxy traitors, I hope you get cancer.

[*Aside*] And that's what I did.

Catholic Women's University College. *Enter* JULIET, *above.*

TIM: Juliet … Juliet …

JULIET: What?

TIM: I need to use your phone.

JULIET: Tim, the nuns will shit if they find you here. They'll think you're from the boys' college.

TIM: Do you have a phone in your dorm?

JULIET: Come in.

TIM: It's an emergency. It's John.

JULIET: What's wrong?

TIM: I need you to ring him. Our parents have banned us.

JULIET: Arseholes.

TIM: Poxy traitors …I called mine poxy traitors. I need you to call him. They won't suspect a girl.

Enter BOB *before* JOHN.

It's ringing.

BOB: Hello.

JULIET: Hello, it's Juliet calling. May I please speak to John please?

BOB: One moment, Juliet.

JOHN: [*softly*] Hello?

JULIET: Tim just told me. He wants to talk to you.

TIM: Are you okay?

JOHN: [*no*] Yep.

TIM: We'll get through this.

JOHN: [*how?*] Yep.

TIM: We'll be okay. I … I love you.

JOHN: I love you too. I'd better go.

TIM: Bye.

JOHN: Bye.

JOHN *exits.*

TIM: Oh shit. That man's going to destroy his son.

JULIET: Come on. I'll sneak you out through the chapel.

Quadrangle. LEE, *who we will soon know as a campus activist, reads from the Monash University student newspaper.*

LEE: *Lot's Wife*: Monash Uni Student Rag, 1978.
'Dear Editor,
I am gay and the current level of anti-gay thinking on campus surprises me. Gays are just like everyone else. My boyfriend is gay and he was captain of the football team at school. He isn't like the gay stereotype. Us being together for the last three years has never hurt anyone. Don't they know we love each other?
—Paris. First-year medicine.'

TIM, LEE *and* WOODY *have milkshakes.* ROSE *hasn't been given a milkshake.*

WOODY: I just wish members would stop casting themselves in Shakespeare and propose a show to actually challenge the status quo.

LEE: Bourgeois shits.

WOODY: Practical revolutionary theatre. You know what I mean?

TIM: Have you read this letter in *Lot's Wife*?

WOODY: Completely politically naive.

TIM: Isn't it.

LEE: So how's *Blithe Spirit* going, Tim?

TIM: Not very good. I'm just backstage operating the poltergeist effects. Everyone can see me running around in my blacks. I hope I get a role where I'm supposed to be seen soon.

LEE: You will. Student theatre's completely democratic.

TIM: Thanks for the milkshake, Lee.

LEE: S'okay.

TIM: I wrote that letter in *Lot's Wife*.

WOODY: You?

LEE: I thought you were doing science.

TIM: I didn't feel brave enough to sign my real name.

LEE: Some poor first-year med student just got outed.

WOODY: Are you really in a relationship like that?

TIM: Exactly like that.

LEE: Must have been a baby when you met. It's so sweet.

WOODY: It's so encouraging. It's what we're fighting for.

TIM: Where?

WOODY: At Gaysoc.

TIM: What's Gaysoc?

WOODY: I thought that's why you were sitting here.

LEE: Haven't you come here for the meeting?

TIM: What meeting?

LEE: Campus Gays. You must join.

TIM: If it means I'll meet other gay people because I only know you guys from the Drama Society.

WOODY: Well there is some crossover with the Drama Society.

LEE: It's just me and Woody. We're Gaysoc.

WOODY: And Rose.

LEE: Oh yeah. Have you met? This is Rose.

TIM: Hello. How are you?

WOODY: So, the minutes should show we started at one thirty-four p.m.

LEE: With the struggle for the betterment of gay and lesbian life on the table—

WOODY: Woody presiding, Lee as secretary—

LEE: And where's the mini skirt I was promised?

WOODY: Don't be sexist.

LEE: Was I?

WOODY: Borderline. And Tim. We have our new member Tim. Welcome.

TIM: Thanks.

LEE: And we all have swamp-water milkshakes because I'm so generous.

WOODY: Lime and Chocolate, who would have thought?

LEE: Thank you.

WOODY: Keep the receipts.

LEE: They're on me.

WOODY: Good. So. Sexuality week.

LEE: We would like to have a couple kissing in the lift in the Menzies building.

WOODY: But we don't have one; no couple has volunteered.

LEE: Woody? You and Peter?

WOODY: My boyfriend? The nurse? Like he'd do anything radical?

LEE: Well. What about Tim and his boyfriend?

TIM: No. I don't think so.

LEE: Well, there are eighteen thousand kids on campus and if we believe the statistics of one in ten that means nearly two thousand gay guys. And girls. So where are they? And don't say the library toilets.

WOODY: It's too confronting for them to come to a group like this.

ROSE: Have you thought about it being a couple of women kissing in the lift?

LEE: Yes.

TIM: [*as Queen Victoria*] Surely that doesn't happen.

ROSE: What?

TIM: I was being Queen Victoria.

ROSE: Oh right. To be funny?

TIM: Um. Yes.

WOODY: Rose's big beef is lesbian invisibility.

ROSE: Are you speaking for me?

WOODY: No. Rose, maybe you should run a workshop about it.

ROSE: Maybe you should. It's not my job.

WOODY: Okay, well, I'd be happy to run one on lesbian invisibility but—

ROSE: Sure. You do that.

TIM: Rose, I'm sorry if—I was out of line.

ROSE: Do you actually care or is this movement just about you men cruising?

LEE: Ah, I actually take offense to that, actually.

ROSE: Do you? Because actually what we talk about at these meetings is men: how that-guy-over-there's jeans sit or how you can glimpse brown nipples and lithe skin showing from his bib-and-brace overalls.

LEE: Well.

ROSE: There are actually women and men with no where to turn, actually, and they've been brutalised by parents and institutions crushing and actually trying to destroy them. How is Gaysoc going to reach them, really reach them and not just their bums?

TIM: What about a hotline?

ROSE: What?

TIM: Just, um, people could phone up if they have questions. About being gay. My boyfriend would never kiss me in the lifts. That's not his bag but he's having these troubles with his Dad 'brutalising' and all those things you say—and if there was an anonymous phone line, the Johns out there might make contact. I might phone that number too.

WOODY: Sort of thing that the union could help us set up. I know the counselor. She could train us.

TIM: Right. Yeah. Rose, what do you think?

ROSE: I think … Having a hotline to call might have helped … when my dad kicked me out of home.

TIM: [*aside*] My very first Gaysoc meeting and I was elected deputy chair of a sub-committee.

Juliet's house. JOHN *runs to* JULIET *and* TIM.

JULIET: Here he is.

JOHN: Fuck.

TIM: John? Where have you been?

JULIET: We didn't know where you were, John.

JOHN: I ran.

TIM: You're sweating. Did you run the whole way?

JOHN: I ran. I bolted. I'm dead. I'm fuckin' … Dad and I had a fight. What am I doing here? He'll work out I'm here. He knows you're here, Tim.

TIM: What can he do?

JULIET: My mum's making you dinner.

JOHN: I should go back. He knows you're a friend of Juliet's. He'll work it out, Tim.

JOHN *kicks something.*

TIM: John—

JOHN: I just cracked. I've never spoken to him like that, never spoken to anyone like that. I called him an arsehole, Tim. I told him if he can't accept you and me, I don't want him to be my father and then I just took off.

TIM: I think that's good.

JOHN: It's my dad. Don't say that. It's my dad, Tim.

Enter MARIE, *pursued by* BOB CALEO.

BOB: Is this Juliet?

MARIE: This is her mother speaking. Hello.

BOB: This is Robert Caleo. John's father.

MARIE: Oh hello Robert. Now we've found John. He's standing right here.

JULIET *signals.*

But. No. He's not.

BOB: Is Tim there?

MARIE: Tim? Oh.

The signals grow.

Lovely. Well …

BOB: Do you realise there are homosexuals at your dinner table?

MARIE: Oh, look. I don't think it's any of your business, Robert. You're being a fool. My beetroot soup is ready to serve and I'd prefer that you didn't ring here again. Goodnight.

BOB *exits.*

Well. I'm sorry, John, but your father is a very rude and irritating man.

JOHN: Sorry.

MARIE: No. That's alright, love.

JOHN *and* TIM *are clinging to each other.*

Oh. Juliet, you make up the spare room. It's only a single bed, boys—I'm sorry.

MARIE *exits.*

JOHN: I won't be able to stay, Juliet.

JULIET: You must stay. You've done the hardest part.

JULIET *exits.*

JOHN: Dad'll be waiting up.

TIM: Serves him right don't you think?

JOHN: I know it's wrong, but I really enjoyed giving him the shits today.

TIM: Stay.

Silence.

JOHN: Okay.

TIM: Will you marry me? Err, why did I say that? That just fell out.

JOHN: It's nice. You're a dick but it's nice, Timba.

TIM: 'Timba'? I like that.

[*Aside*] That night we fucked on Marie's divan like we were reclaiming old territory.

The students' union office. WOODY *and* TIM *share a beanbag.*

WOODY: Might be a problem with the phone.

TIM: I tested it.

WOODY: It might take some time before people feel empowered enough to call.

TIM: Oh okay.

WOODY: Yeah.

TIM: I told John about the Homosexual Conference.

WOODY: Oh good. Will he come?

TIM: He's even keen to get a homo group started at his college.

WOODY: Gay group.

TIM: Oh okay. I think it's his dad. John's getting political—and empowered.

WOODY: My boyfriend doesn't get it. I thought Peter doing nursing was somehow political but it's not; he just wants to be a nurse. Peter thinks activists are just angry people. I organise rallies; he invites friends to tennis parties.

TIM: John's sporty. You don't hear of many sporty gay guys.

WOODY: Gotta keep fit.

TIM: Woody, you know when you're making love … ?

WOODY: Do you mean fucking? You're talking about anal sex?

TIM: Have you done it?

WOODY: Many times. I think it's important. Men being intimate or being penetrated challenges the patriarchy.

TIM: Oh okay. Yeah—

WOODY: Have you?

TIM: John screwed me for the first time last night and I found it painful. I'd done it to him but this time he did me and it would hardly go in and it felt like I needed a shit.

WOODY: It takes practice, my friend. You've just got to relax … I get Peter to chew my earlobe. It distracts me and before I know it, he's in.

TIM: Weird. John too.

WOODY: Might have to meet this John.

TIM: Thanks for that.

WOODY: It's a counselling line after all.

TIM: Wish the phone would ring.

The phone doesn't ring.

One more thing, my bum wouldn't close and the cum kept dribbling out for about half an hour.

WOODY *calculates his response.*

WOODY: Your sphincter was probably in shock. It'll get used to it.

TIM: It's a bit sad to have lovemaking with John reduced to dick-in-the-bum mechanics.

WOODY: Fucking. Call it fucking.

TIM: Oh okay. I would like you to meet John.

WOODY: I don't believe it's fair to expect our lovers to fulfill all our needs.

TIM: But does your boyfriend agree?

WOODY: Peter likes to play tennis and I don't, so he plays with other people. It's the same with sex.

TIM: Where do you meet gay guys?

WOODY: University. Gay bars. I think you'd like Peter. Sinewy and lithe—a seriously sexy man.

TIM *and* WOODY *are gradually drawn close as they fantasise about their boyfriends.*

TIM: John is the most beautiful man I have ever seen. His chest is round and his eyes are like chocolate.

WOODY: Mine's Mediterranean too.

TIM: I don't think I could ever go to Italy—it might kill me.

WOODY: Catholic boys' school must have been interesting. Did you have a sexual relationship then?

TIM: Yes.

WOODY: Do you remember the first time?

TIM: Of course.

WOODY: I had an erection for most of my schooling.

TIM: Father Wallbridge organised a retreat to Barwon Heads. John and I put our sleeping bags together and nuzzled noses. He smelled so sweet. I remember exchanging breath and his puffing. I made him cum twice and he said he felt like he'd played a grand final. I wrote a poem the next day about two suns exchanging atmospheres, drawn into each other, spiraling into each other.

WOODY: Can I kiss you?

TIM: Sorry. You can't.

WOODY: Okay.

> ***A gay bar.*** JOHN *and* TIM *approach the* DOOR-BITCH. TIM *has a newspaper.*

DOOR-BITCH: Hi, boys. Hold on to your raffle ticket; there's a lucky door prize.

> TIM *and* JOHN *venture in.*

[*To his colleague*] Daisy, tell me you saw those eyelashes. And they're real.

> *Gays for days.*

TIM / JOHN: My God.

TIM: I didn't expect it to look like this.

JOHN: Where do we sit? There?

TIM: No they're kissing there.

JOHN: Don't stare.

TIM: Shit.

JOHN: Over near the bar.

TIM: They're actually all gay men.

JOHN: Well yeah.

TIM: Let's start talking to people.

JOHN: What, 'We're Tim and John and we'd like to be your friends'?

TIM: I want to go up to them and say 'So, do your parents know?' 'How did they take it?' 'Tell me about your life.'

JOHN: Looks like a lot of their parents wouldn't be still alive.

TIM: They even had this in the foyer [*the newspaper*].

JOHN: A poofter newspaper?

TIM: Gay newspaper. That's what you say. Or homosexual.

An old QUEEN *has approached.*

QUEEN ONE: You boys new here?

TIM: Yes.

QUEEN ONE: Didn't think I'd seen you. I'm sure I'd remember.

TIM: Maybe there are other clubs.

TIM *searches for a listing in the newspaper.*

JOHN: Stay.

TIM: Here?

JOHN: Stay over tonight.

TIM: No way.

JOHN: Stay. Mum and Dad don't get back from the beach-house until Monday. You can if you want. Bring your newspaper.

TIM: Come off it. [*Reading*] Look there are other gay bars … and gay dentists.

JOHN: Stay.

TIM: There's an advert here for a gay plumber.

JOHN: So are you going to stay?

TIM: No. I'm not. What if they come home early?

JOHN: They never do. Please.

TIM: Oh let's just do it in the car.

JOHN: Just stay.

TIM: No. I'm buying you a drink.

A BARTENDER *pops up.*

BARTENDER: What can I get you girls?

JOHN: Us? Oh. Beer?

BARTENDER: Drinks at the other bar. We do toasted sandwiches and coffee.

JOHN: Oh.

A second QUEEN *drifts by.*

QUEEN TWO: Grab a hot buttered man on toast, sweets.

JOHN: A what?

BARTENDER: Fresh out, lovey.

DOOR-BITCH: Oh. Story of my life.

TIM: Hey?

TIM *and* JOHN *try to understand the gay prattle.*

BARTENDER: Ooh ah. Barbra Streisand Babs Babs.

JOHN: [*to* TIM] What are they talking about?

QUEEN TWO: [*to* BARTENDER] A Star is Born. Such a sell out. Quack quack darling la la, Ducky.

TIM: [*to* JOHN] I can't work it out.

BARTENDER: [*to* QUEEN TWO] I know. Mmwa mmwa tee hee ha ha babs babs Judy Judy vagina.

JOHN: [*to* TIM] Should we dance?

QUEEN TWO: Rock-Hudson-dizzy-bitch-fist.

TIM: [*to* JOHN] People will stare.

JOHN *pecks a kiss on* TIM.

Fuck it, okay, I'll stay, let's go to your place.

LOIS *is heard approaching them.*

LOIS: Paul, bring in the blue bag please.

JOHN: Shit. Mum.

The gays in the gay bar scream and run away because we are now at ***the Caleo home****.*

TIM: They've come home early?

JOHN: Shit. Put your clothes in the cupboard.

LOIS: The blue bag in the boot please.

JOHN: Get in the cupboard too.

TIM *hides. Enter* LOIS.

Mum.

LOIS: Hello, dear. Will you help your brother get the things in please?

JOHN: Mum. Tim's here.

LOIS: John …

JOHN: Is Dad here?

LOIS: Probably on his way in. He went to put the bins out.

JOHN: Sorry.

LOIS: Look you'd jolly well better get Tim out. Not very happy about this.

JOHN: Don't tell Dad. Please, Mum.

LOIS: Honestly, I think the whole thing's absurd but don't disobey your father.

JOHN: We're in love.

LOIS: I don't judge you, John. I'm just afraid. I'll go busy your father with something or other.

JOHN: Thank you.

The Fifth National Australian Homosexual Conference.

TIM *takes* JOHN*'s hand.*

TIM: [*aside*] We climbed the stairs toward the Universal Workshop at Monash University. John took my hand as we entered The Fifth National Annual Australian Homosexual Conference.

[*To* JOHN] Don't mention Peter to Woody.

JOHN: Why?

TIM: They broke up.

JOHN: No?

TIM: Keep up, our friends are sluts. Peter's seeing some gorgeous guy from his nursing course.

JOHN: We're playing tennis with Peter next weekend.

TIM: Don't mention that to Woody. I want to hear about both their rebound sex.

JOHN: Tim?

TIM: Have you noticed how many spunks there are at this conference?

JOHN: Tim, are you trying to hurt my feelings?

TIM: How is that hurting your feelings?

JOHN: You say too much.

TIM: I do not say too much, John. I just worry sometimes, sometimes I worry that we're missing out …

JOHN: On what?

TIM: … on what people our age are experiencing. They all go on about it: Screech Beach changing sheds, saunas, trade—

JOHN: That's saying too much.

TIM: No, I mean, well, I'm nearly twenty-one and, you know, I feel sexually inexperienced. Don't you feel that? You've only had sex with me.

JOHN: I don't want to have sex with other people.

TIM: Okay.

JOHN: Is it okay?

TIM: Yes. But would you allow me to?

JOHN: I don't know why you'd want to. Is it something about me?

TIM: 'I don't believe it's fair to expect our lovers to fulfil all our needs.'

JOHN: Where d'you read that?

TIM: An open relationship isn't a sin, John.

JOHN: I don't want to talk about this. Not here in public.

JOHN *brushes roughly past* TIM *to exit.*

TIM: [*aside*] I think that was a no.

Enter HARRY.

HARRY: Do you have the time?

TIM: [*aside*] In my search for adventure, however, I did start trolling. [*To* HARRY] It's eleven.

They're at ***a party****.*

HARRY: Are you a poofter?

TIM: Um yeah.

HARRY: This is my first gay party. God, if my parents knew! In their country they used to stone people for being gay.

TIM: I'm pretty stoned.

HARRY: I'm just drunk on being here. I can't believe how many good-looking guys there are. What time is it?

TIM: Twelve thirty.

HARRY: I've missed my train.

TIM: I live in St Kilda in a share house. I have a spare mattress.

HARRY: I have to get home before my parents wake up.

TIM: It's two. How early do they get up?

HARRY: Six. Still two hours. Does anal sex hurt?

TIM: Only at first.

HARRY: I'm a virgin and I reckon you'd be gentle with me.

TIM: You're sweet, but I have a boyfriend.

HARRY: He's not here. You don't think I'm attractive?

TIM: I'm trying to resist. Believe me.

HARRY: I'm getting ball cramp waiting all this time.

TIM: [*aside*] I screwed Harry. He had no trouble doing what, for me, had been a painful thing. In fact he enjoyed it immensely.

HARRY *climaxes.*

[*To* HARRY] Have you done this before? Was this all a con-job?

HARRY: Come off it. Shit, my parents will be up in a second. Bye.

HARRY *exits and we are immediately at ...*

NEW ROMANTIC: Hi.

Inflation Nightclub *with a* NEW ROMANTIC *in a powdered wig.*

TIM: First time here?

NEW ROMANTIC: No.

TIM: Cool.

NEW ROMANTIC: New Romantic nights are the best at Inflation.

TIM: Cool.

NEW ROMANTIC: Lee told you I liked you, hey?

TIM: No.

NEW ROMANTIC: He did. I do.

TIM: Oh.

[*Aside*] Philip was clearly an experienced lover. He manoeuvred himself around my cock with obvious expertise. Again, I sensed that something was missing. I didn't know what.

NEW ROMANTIC: So do you want to go out with me?

TIM: No.

NEW ROMANTIC: Why not?

TIM: It was really nice but I couldn't bear it if my boyfriend found out.

NEW ROMANTIC: Maybe you should have thought about that before you led me on.

TIM: I didn't lead you on. I was honest the whole way.

NEW ROMANTIC: Cock-sucker.

NEW ROMANTIC *exits. Instantly ...*

Franco's bedroom *with* FRANCO.

TIM: All I ever do is upset people.

FRANCO: What would your boyfriend do if he found out about our fling?

TIM: Part of me wants to share it with him.

FRANCO: Come off it. Christ, we're gonna be early at this rate.

TIM: John's my best friend. I've shared everything with him. You look good in my shirt.

FRANCO: This whole month behind his back?

TIM: I can't. Oh I can't wear this.

TIM *changes his shirt.*

He loves me so much, everyone says that, but I feel obligated to him and I want craziness.

FRANCO: Sounds like you've got some issues there, mister. When my boy gets back from overseas he won't know shit. Shit, let's wait. I don't want to be on time.

TIM: Knowing that this, you and me, was always going to be finite has made it so intense.

FRANCO: You wanna fuck again, hey.

TIM: Yep.

FRANCO: Me too. We're late anyway.

FRANCO *exits. Instantly …*

PETER: Where's John tonight, Tim?

A party. PETER *is near* TIM.

TIM: What'd you say, Peter?

PETER: Is John coming later?

TIM: Wanna go upstairs or something, Peter? Party's too loud.

PETER: I'm right. So John still not here?

TIM: Has some nerdy chiro assignment.

PETER: You're still together?

TIM: Yeah.

PETER: Yeah.

TIM: You heard John and I had a spat at your tennis thing?

PETER: Yeah.

TIM: Yeah.

PETER: Yeah and you seem to be coming onto me on the dance floor all night.

TIM: Yeah.

PETER: Yeah.

TIM: Thinning out now. I might go home soon. Wanna come round for a drink?

PETER: Sure, but not for sex. I couldn't do it to John.
TIM: He doesn't have to know. You're not rejecting me are you?
PETER: I wouldn't feel right about it.
TIM: Oh. Okay. Don't tell John. Okay?

PETER *exits. And immediately ...*

Tim's house *in St Kilda.* TIM *and* JOHN *are in bed.*

JOHN: Tell me, Tim.
TIM: What?
JOHN: There's something on your mind.
TIM: Not now.
JOHN: Just say it. There's something—
TIM: It's not something I want to say in bed.
JOHN: Don't torture me, Tim.
TIM: I need some space.
JOHN: What's that mean?
TIM: We've been together for five years and I'm starting to lose my identity. I'm no longer Tim but part of John and Tim.
JOHN: What's wrong with that?
TIM: I want to go to acting school next year and there are just things, things that I want to do that wouldn't involve you.
JOHN: You mean sex with other men.
TIM: I mean a separation. A trial separation.
JOHN: How long for?
TIM: A couple of months.
JOHN: When does this start?
TIM: Well, I don't know.
JOHN: Now?
TIM: Well yes, I guess it has to start now.
JOHN: I see.
TIM: Are you okay about it?
JOHN: No, why would I be? Can I still sleep here tonight?
TIM: Of course. I'm not going to kick you out of my bed.
JOHN: Well if it's started I can—
TIM: No, stay tonight.
JOHN: Yeah. I would prefer to stay tonight.
TIM: Yeah. Stay tonight but then tomorrow we'll start a separation.

JOHN: Tomorrow we start?
TIM: Starts tonight but stay tonight. If you like. I don't—
JOHN: A trial though.
TIM: Yeah, for a set time. A few months.
JOHN: No more Tim and John.
TIM: Just for a few months.
JOHN: It doesn't mean we can't cuddle.
TIM: I think it does.

JOHN *turns his back on* TIM.

[*Aside*] I hoped to God you wouldn't start crying. Later, Juliet told me he cried daily.

TIM *places a hand on* JOHN. *He shrugs it away.*

[*Aside*] I lay awake for ages.

JOHN *takes* TIM*'s hand and wraps it around himself.*

A DIRECTOR *and some acting candidates are watching* TIM ...

... at ***the National Institute of Dramatic Art****, in an audition room.*

DIRECTOR: Tim mate, good. When you're ready we'll hear your audition. You look tired, mate. When you're ready. Don't be nervous.
TIM: Okay. Ready?
DIRECTOR: Ready mate.
TIM: 'When the phone—'
DIRECTOR: Sorry mate, before you start. We saw you last year, didn't we?
TIM: Yes. Told me to come back.
DIRECTOR: Just wanted to check. When you're ready.

TIM *recites the following as his monologue.*

TIM: When the phone call came, things shook. 'Tim, you're in.' I'm in. I am in. An actor friend from Anthill says, 'That's good, turtle, if that's what you want.' What I want? Is she mad? I wanted to tell everybody, the woman in the café, the old man in the street, but I also didn't want to appear to be bragging. 'A cappuccino thanks, and by the way, I just got into NIDA.' [*As a friend of his mum*] 'Very proud. Mum just told me, you've been accepted into Narnia.'

Narnia? For fuck's sake. It's the school Mel Gibson went to and Judy Davis. Haven't you heard of it? I went and got a crew cut. A new start. Regrowth.

TIM *removes his wig to reveal a shaved head. The monologue becomes a duologue between* JOHN *and* TIM *at* TIM*'s flat.* TIM *mimes the kettle and the popcorn as though he is performing the scene in a rehearsal room at NIDA. The* DIRECTOR *and* ACTORS *remain on stage observing.*

JOHN: [*entering*] I don't know if I like your hair.

JOHN*'s hair has reached its 1980s height.*

TIM: Number two. I like it. Cup of tea? I'm making popcorn. Want some?

TIM *starts the detailed business of making a cup of tea.*

JOHN: Just tea. Please.
TIM: Kettle's on.

TIM *makes sure the mimed kettle is on at the wall.*

So dumb barely seeing you the past month. Surprised you came. Glad you came. Just busy packing and …
JOHN: I came to congratulate you. Juliet told me.
TIM: Thanks. I'm over the moon.
JOHN: We made you something. I'm not going to see you much am I?
TIM: I'll be coming back from Sydney for the term breaks.
JOHN: Guess so.

TIM *tends to the popcorn.*

So, I've been seeing someone.
TIM: You have?
JOHN: Yeah.
TIM: Anyone I know?
JOHN: Peter.
TIM: Lucky you. He's sweet. And very cute. I tried once but he couldn't do it because of you. That's what he said.
JOHN: He told me.
TIM: Have you slept together?
JOHN: A couple of times. Mostly we play tennis.

TIM: What's he like in bed?

JOHN: You're not even jealous.

TIM: No. I'm not. Is that why you told me?

JOHN: Maybe. I don't know. Yes.

TIM *pours the kettle into the popcorn.*

TIM: I think it's great, a chance to experience something different.

JOHN: Did you just … ? You just poured the kettle into the popcorn.

TIM: [*has given himself away*] Yes. Yes, I did.

JOHN: Oh. Don't go away.

TIM *completes the detailed task of disposing of the popcorn and preparing the cups of tea. He wipes up after himself as he talks.*

TIM: Come off it. What about Peter?

JOHN: Dad scared him off anyway.

TIM: Bob? Finally on my side.

TIM *sips his mimed cup of tea—careful, it might be hot.*

JOHN: I'll miss you too much.

TIM: I'm shit scared. I know that I'm going to rock up on the day and then they'll go:

DIRECTOR: 'Hey listen, I thought Tim Conigrave was the boy with the blonde curly hair, not the poof trying to look masculine in James Dean gear.' Sorry mate. Keep on going.

TIM: [*distracted by the reappearance of the* DIRECTOR] Right, ahh … Maybe I just fluked my way in on the day.

JOHN: You're such a worry-wart. We made you this.

JOHN *produces a scrapbook.* TIM *puts down his tea and looks through it. The scrapbook is the first real object in the scene.*

This is what we made you.

TIM: What's … '*This Is Your Life*—actually only the last five years.' How did you get all this together?

JOHN: The others pitched in. Biscuit did the section on skating stacks.

TIM: Classic.

JOHN: Down the freeway ramp. Juliet had the piccies of the plays.

TIM: And Christmas Eve on the Yarra. All with commentary. Your handwriting. You loop your lowercase 'l's like we were told to.

JOHN: Do I?

TIM: Thank you. Thanks, John.

JOHN: No wuckers.

TIM: I want to make one for you.

JOHN: Like you'll have time in the next three years.

TIM: What am I getting myself in for?

JOHN: I want to buy you something.

TIM: What?

JOHN: I don't know. A ring.

TIM: A ring?

JOHN: Yeah. A ring. A kind of memento to say thanks for the last five years.

TIM: Well, I'd like to buy you one too. Most couples give each other rings at the start of the relationship, and here we are doing it when we break up.

JOHN: Are we breaking up?

TIM: Well …

JOHN: I thought we were just separating, a trial, just seeing other people.

TIM: I think NIDA's changed that. It'll be hard to maintain anything over such a distance. I'm sorry, John, but don't you think the relationship was winding down?

JOHN: Do you always have to tell the truth?

TIM: It was getting a bit stale.

JOHN: Shit. Well, I guess I knew this was coming. Let's get on a tram and …

TIM: Where to?

JOHN: I don't want to go home. Let's go to Inflation. Wednesday's Gay Night.

> ***Inflation Nightclub.*** JOHN *and* TIM *let loose on a crowded dance floor to something like Depeche Mode's 'Just Can't Get Enough'.*

TIM: It's like we're on our first date.

JOHN: Pardon?

TIM: Nothing.

JOHN: Hey?

TIM: I want to kiss you, but I can't—

JOHN: I can't hear you, Tim.

TIM: I know. Doesn't matter. I do love you, John Caleo.

The other dancers dissipate and for a moment it is just TIM *and* JOHN.

[*Aside*] We bought the rings.

And then it is just TIM.

I put mine on my wedding finger.

The music takes us to ...

—INTERVAL—

ACT TWO

The National Institute of Dramatic Art. ACTORS *in black lycra are warming up on stage.*

TEACHER: On the count of three, form a new friendship. One. Two. Three.

The ACTORS *do as they are told.*

Now separate. Form a new friendship. And separate. Form a new one. Good. Keep that repeating, okay, for three years.

Roll on the floor. And cry. Cry on a neighbour. Good. And totally breaking down. Okay, shake it out. Very good. Thoughts?

AN ACTOR: Um, it's like the friends you make here will be your friends for life.

TEACHER: Anyone else feel that?

ALL: Yes.

AN ACTOR: And it's like, it's like some people have a block with anger.

She death-stares the culprit.

TEACHER: Okay, good, choose an animal and just—

AN ACTOR: I'm a monkey.

AN ACTOR: I'm a monkey.

AN ACTOR: I'm a chimpanzee.

AN ACTOR: I'm a Central African fruit-gathering gibbon.

TEACHER: Ah, Tim, effeminate monkeys don't get work.

TIM *masculinises his monkey—more a gorilla cruising.*

They all fight and fuck as excited monkeys do.

JOHN *interrupts the scene.*

JOHN: How's drama school?

TIM *stops being a monkey. The* ACTORS *become a car.* TIM *and* JOHN *drive together.*

TIM: It's all I talk about.

JOHN: Oh.

JOHN *adjust the rear-vision mirror—an* ACTOR*'s hand. The* ACTORS *also provide the hum of the engine.*

TIM: I can't escape it. How's chiropractics?

JOHN: I'm doing pretty well. We can stop at a servo soon if you want.

TIM: Good to have someone to drive home with.

JOHN: I wanted to check out Sydney.

JOHN *shifts the gear stick—another* ACTOR*'s foot.*

No air-conditioning sorry.

TIM: I'll make air-conditioning with my coffee cup.

TIM *winds down the window. An* ACTOR *provides the handle and noise. Another* ACTOR *blows the incoming breeze.* TIM *shovels air in with his empty coffee cup.*

JOHN: You're still mad.

JOHN *turns on the indicator. A corner.*

TIM: John, you deserve better than me.

JOHN: You think?

TIM: I don't deserve you at all. But I would like us to get back together. If you'll have me back.

JOHN: Good.

TIM: Good?

JOHN: Yeah.

TIM: Bit understated.

JOHN: No. I think that's good.

TIM: Right.

An ice-cream van is heard passing.

JOHN: My parents want me to stay in Melbourne but, maybe, when you graduate we should try living together, maybe.

TIM: In Sydney?

JOHN: I guess.

TIM: And what about now?

JOHN: I don't know.

TIM: I mean the phone-calls alone and long distance relationships don't work …

JOHN: Suppose.

TIM: Maybe it means while we're apart we can have sex outside the relationship?

JOHN: So it's a relationship?

TIM: Yeah. But apart.

The car drives JOHN *away.* TIM *fucks the nearest male* ACTOR.

FUCK ACTOR: So I said to Betty, I'm not coming to voice class if we can't take our shoes off.

TIM: Sorry can we just, sorry, NIDA's all I talk about.

FUCK ACTOR: Sorry, yeah, keep on fucking me.

TIM: Thanks.

TEACHER: Anyone else feel that?

ACTORS / TIM: No. / Yes.

TEACHER: Work hard Tim. And don't wear those sneakers so much. You came up at a Heads of Department meeting and we don't think they let your feet breathe.

TIM: No. Okay. Thanks.

TEACHER: Breathe.

A monkey screams. TIM *drinks some water. An* ACTOR *approaches* TIM. *It's their water bottle he's drinking from.*

ACTOR: That's for my voice. I have nodules.

TIM: Sorry. Thought it was mine.

TIM *offers her the water bottle.*

ACTOR: It's fine actually. You have it.

TIM: Are you afraid that you might catch—

ACTOR: No.

TIM: I might be gay but I don't have AIDS.

ACTOR: I know. It's just …

TIM: It's what? Even if I did, you can't get it from sharing a drink.

The ACTORS *scurry from* TIM *as screaming monkeys.*

On stage, ***the Stables Theatre****.* TIM *addresses Members' Night.*

My name's Tim. Tim Conigrave and, um, I'm a new member here at the Griffin—Griffin Theatre Company—and I think it's really good that someone like me can just get up and say my idea at Members' Night … tonight. I just graduated from NIDA, the class of '84, so

I know some of you … I have seen some really interesting things here and even though the seats are so uncomfortable you don't notice, um, but some of you are fidgeting so just … I'll be down in the foyer with you all so just talk to me um if you don't think my thing is shit. But what I'm proposing is a devised response, not that I'm a writer, I'm an actor, but a response to HIV AIDS which will … because the media doesn't deal with stories about people affected except the sex-death-horror shit, which is fucked, so maybe we can do something. I heard this military general talking about the Namibian Border War on Radio National and he called civilians soft targets and maybe a good working title for this project could be *Soft Targets*.

A VOICE FROM THE AUDIENCE: Sounds a bit like an anus.

TIM: Oh well maybe you'd prefer *Fuck Me Dead*, y'wanker … I'll be in the foyer.

Albion Street Clinic. *Enter two* DOCTORS.

DOCTOR ONE: John 2118.

DOCTOR TWO: Tim 2117.

TIM *and* JOHN *go to separate consulting rooms. Their* DOCTORS *speak in unison.*

DOCTOR ONE / DOCTOR TWO: How do you define your sexuality: heterosexual, homosexual, bisexual, transsexual?

JOHN / TIM: Homosexual. / Gay.

DOCTOR ONE / DOCTOR TWO: Do you practice anal sex?

JOHN / TIM: Yes. / Practice makes perfect.

DOCTOR ONE / DOCTOR TWO: Okay, and are you active or passive?

JOHN / TIM: Well, both. / Kinda, both.

DOCTOR ONE / DOCTOR TWO: If versatile, what ratio?

JOHN / TIM: Oh … Well … Fifty fifty. / Twenty eighty. Mostly a top.

DOCTOR ONE / DOCTOR TWO: Are you in a relationship?

JOHN / TIM: Yes. / Yes.

DOCTOR ONE / DOCTOR TWO:Would you say it was monogamous?

JOHN / TIM: Yes. / Um, well, no.

DOCTOR ONE / DOCTOR TWO: How many women have you had sex with in the last six months?

JOHN / TIM: None. / None.

DOCTOR ONE / DOCTOR TWO: How many men?

JOHN / TIM: One. / Some. Three? Some.

DOCTOR ONE / DOCTOR TWO: Have you paid for sex in the past month?

JOHN / TIM: No. I haven't. / Sauna? Not this month.

DOCTOR ONE / DOCTOR TWO: Okay. I need to also ask you how you would feel in two weeks if I told you that you were positive.

TIM: I'm involved in a theatre project about AIDS …

JOHN: I would be devastated.

TIM: … so I know it's not a death sentence.

DOCTOR ONE / DOCTOR TWO: What support mechanisms do you have?

JOHN / TIM: My boyfriend. / My boyfriend.

DOCTOR TWO: [*to* TIM] Okay, because I'm afraid your glands were up all over your body. I'll take some blood now.

TIM *and* JOHN *are leaving the clinic together.*

JOHN: [*to* TIM] Probably just the flu. Mine weren't up.

TIM: Yeah. I'm not bothered.

JOHN: Should we walk to Oxford Street for lunch?

There's a bounce in TIM*'s step.*

TIM: Sure.

JOHN: Not like that.

TIM: What? Shut up. I just had an AIDS test. I'm a fast-lane gay now.

He moves as a fast-lane gay moves.

A Sydney living room. *Enter* RICHARD, *an AIDS patient, a large grotesque puppet with an empty frame and sunken cheeks, coughing and spluttering. He holds a drip stand. Tubes dangle.*

RICHARD: I have a recurring one. My boat has broken down in the Congo but everyone else gets a nice little boat ride. I have to walk through this jungle with snakes and spiders and quicksand. When I fall into it someone pulls me out but I always sink back in. People drop supplies from a helicopter but it can't land. I'm angry and lonely. But I learn a lot. I see a gorilla having a baby. Everyone has seen a gorilla in a book but the actual experience is something else.

TIM: We are asking people—

RICHARD: I have night sweats.

TIM: The cast and I made some set questions for our research that we—

RICHARD: I hate having to take morphine. I hate the taste.

TIM: What's it for?

RICHARD: For headaches that nothing else touches. It also helps with the cough.

TIM: You must have good parties.

RICHARD: Oh p-lease. It's not a party drug. It's hideous. It tastes revolting and cuts you out of the world.

RICHARD *has a coughing fit.*

TIM: There's a question—

RICHARD: Space shuttle crashed this morning.

TIM: I saw that.

RICHARD: School teacher died in it.

TIM: That's right. There's a question we're asking everyone we interview for the theatre project. Is there a message about living with AIDS that you want people to know?

RICHARD: I don't think I'll get to see your play.

Albion Street Clinic. DOCTOR TWO *approaches* TIM.

DOCTOR TWO: Tim 2117. Thanks. Take a seat, Tim. Tim, I'm sorry to inform you that you are positive.

TIM: Shit, you're kidding.

DOCTOR TWO: This is the result sheet.

TIM: It's not that I don't believe you, but my boyfriend was just told he's negative.

DOCTOR TWO: Right. And obviously you have a sexual relationship with him?

TIM: For nine years.

DOCTOR TWO: Okay. Well … I'll just ask you to return outside. I'll just need a moment.

Waiting room. TIM *approaches* JOHN.

JOHN: Tim?

TIM: John.

JOHN: Tim.

TIM: John …

JOHN: What?

TIM: I'm positive.

JOHN: But I'm negative.

TIM: The doctors are yelling. Why? They're yelling.

DOCTOR TWO *approaches.*

DOCTOR TWO: Tim and John, would you both like to come in please …

Consulting room. *Instantaneous.*

… Thank you. John. I'm sorry. You have been given the wrong result.

TIM: No.

DOCTOR TWO: You are in fact positive, John. I'm terribly sorry. I should explain. If your result is negative you see a counsellor, and if you are positive you see a doctor. The clerk put your file in the wrong pigeonhole and the counsellor gave you the result without checking it. I am terribly sorry. This should not happen. I am truly so sorry. I want to take some blood from both of you and do a cell count. John, if you would like to come lie on the bed.

At home. TIM *and* JOHN *are in bed.*

JOHN: How long have we been trying to get to sleep?

TIM: I drifted off before.

JOHN: I have no idea what time it is.

TIM *snakes his head under* JOHN*'s singlet, making him look kind of pregnant.*

TIM: I know you hate it when I do this. I love it. It's so warm. Is it Tuesday or Monday?

JOHN: Dunno. Don't care. Can you not stretch my singlet?

TIM: I'm not. I can hear the little meteorites in your tummy.

JOHN: What does this mean for my business? We've just signed the papers.

TIM: Nothing. It means nothing. You still practise.

JOHN: I tell my business partner.

TIM: But let's limit who we tell. A gay actor's enough let alone an infected poofter looking to be cast. Maybe I thought doing a play about HIV made me immune. *Soft Targets* isn't going great and they want to perform it in the Mardi Gras Festival. They love butcher's paper too much. When that Challenger thing crashed, the NASA thing, the actors all came running in with an idea and they want to start the play set in space with spacemen—and I don't know if that's good. The play might be a disaster.

JOHN: Do you think I infected you?

TIM *doesn't answer.*

The way our cells are, me being more advanced, you with your high T8s—

TIM: It's not important.

JOHN: I just wish I hadn't infected you.

TIM *comes out from under the singlet.*

TIM: We don't know if that's what happened. We can never know. It didn't even have a name. We didn't know it was lurking.

JOHN: Peter's negative and I've only had sex with one other boy. How unlucky can I be?

TIM: Doctors don't know enough about this yet. We're both infected. That's all we know. I have a surprise. Condoms and lube. We are going to welcome them into our family.

JOHN: I don't want to have anal sex, Tim. That's how we got into this mess.

TIM: I'm going to leave the theatre project.

JOHN: Don't.

TIM: I only started it because I was curious. Now that's … It's taking its toll. I have to consider my health now.

JOHN: Are we eighty?

TIM: I'm going to tell the director. We are eighty. All of a sudden … It's hit me now.

JOHN: We're twenty-five.

TIM: I think it's hit me now.

JOHN: Let's try to sleep.

TIM: I don't want to sleep. I want to stay awake for the rest of my life. I want you to hold me. I want my mum to scoop me up and my schoolteachers and all my friends and family … I want everyone to hold me and say it's alright.

JOHN: It's alright, Tim.

TIM: But it's not. We are going to die.

Conigrave home. TIM *is half-dressed in suit pants. His mother is taking up the hem.*

MARY-GERT: I'll kill your father for eating the glacé cherries. Did you see the letters for you? Must update your address. Haven't lived here for years.

TIM: They weren't important.

MARY-GERT: Hold still please, Tim.

TIM: [*re the trouser leg*] Leave it to bag.

MARY-GERT: I didn't know your brother was so much taller. You don't wear a suit, I suppose. Heaven knows how you're paying the bills.

TIM: I got a grant to develop another play.

MARY-GERT: I remember you in *Romeo and Juliet*. You were so beautiful.

TIM: And I'm doing my social work. We're seeing a lot more boys at ACON from other agencies, like STD clinics or the AIDS Bus that works up at The Wall. That's where boy sex-workers find their customers.

MARY-GERT: Oh God. I already have to hide choc-drops from your father and now I'll have to hide all cake ingredients. I'll buy glacé cherries in the morning I suppose. Is John eating here?

TIM: No. At his parent's.

MARY-GERT: I set up the sunroom. If he wants to stay.

TIM: Thank you. Does Anna's fiancé stay in the sunroom?

MARY-GERT: He doesn't stay. Maybe John could pick up some glacé cherries on his way over.

TIM: No. He's had a rough day.

MARY-GERT: He wouldn't mind. Surely. For my fruit cake.

[*Re the hem*] Oh blow, I've done that wrong. I'll re-pin it.

MARY-GERT *re-pins the hem.*

TIM: John was having a big thing with his folks. Send Dad or I'll go.

MARY-GERT: I wouldn't want to trouble anyone; only people are coming round the next day. People from out of town.

TIM: How many functions are we having?

MARY-GERT: Just the normal amount, Tim. She is our only daughter.

Enter DICK.

DICK: Who's our only daughter?

MARY-GERT: Anna, Dick. Ask a silly question.

DICK: How's the suit? Oh yeah. Not bad.

MARY-GERT: Smart.

DICK: Bit of room.

MARY-GERT: No.

DICK: You've lost weight.
TIM: I go to the gym.
DICK: The gym? Well. You box?
TIM: No. Weights.
DICK: Good.
TIM: You ate the glacé cherries.
DICK: Yes.
MARY-GERT: And I'm dark.
DICK: I'll buy more. You get the letters we kept for you?
TIM: Yeah.
DICK: Ought to update your address, mate.
TIM: I have. They're ancient.
DICK: So you, ah, hear we're going to have a spit at the reception?
TIM: Nice.
DICK: In a ballroom.
TIM: Mum said.
DICK: Yeah, over at Ripponlea. No it'll be a big show, don't you worry.
TIM: So it'll be the full deal? The mass and all?
DICK: Yeah. Course.
TIM: Communion and all?
DICK: Yes.
TIM: Is she a Catholic still?
MARY-GERT: Tim.
DICK: And we got an orchestra.
TIM: Jesus.
MARY-GERT: Tim.
DICK: A small chamber orchestra—
TIM: Bit over the top isn't it?
MARY-GERT: Tim.
DICK: She's my only daughter.
TIM: I think it sounds tasteless.
MARY-GERT: Tim.
DICK: Cool it.
TIM: No. This feels like a charade.
DICK: I won't have you destroy this wedding.
MARY-GERT: It's alright, Dick.
TIM: I'm being a jerk. I'm sorry. I'm in a strange—

DICK: If you don't want to be involved then don't be.

DICK *exits.*

MARY-GERT: Thank you, Timothy. Slip them off please.

TIM *takes off the pants.*

Gently. I've pinned that please.

TIM: Sorry.

MARY-GERT: Bite your tongue. I've got relatives arriving from everywhere this week. I don't need stirring.

TIM: I'm not stirring. Ow.

TIM *has stuck himself in the calf with a pin from the hem.*

MARY-GERT: Careful. You stuck yourself.

TIM: It's tiny.

MARY-GERT: Needs Mercurochrome.

TIM: No need and you should use Betadine now.

Enter JOHN.

JOHN: Hello.

TIM: [*to* JOHN] Topolino. [*A nickname*]

MARY-GERT: Hello John, you look sick.

JOHN: No.

MARY-GERT: You're alright?

JOHN: A cold.

MARY-GERT: He doesn't look well.

TIM: He's fine, Mum. Don't fuss.

JOHN: Just had a long day.

MARY-GERT: It's a farce here tonight but you're welcome to join us for dinner. Better get going on it. Heavens, look at the time.

MARY-GERT *exits.*

TIM: It went okay?

JOHN: Yeah.

TIM: What'd they say?

JOHN: Well. Went pretty good. Dad'd already suspected something. He found it strange that we went to Europe five months after I opened the practice.

TIM: Probably relieved you're not pregnant.

JOHN: They asked about my disability insurance, of course. Mum was concerned about my weight and just kept blowing her nose.

TIM: My dad was asking about me losing weight.

JOHN: You haven't.

TIM: Have. At the gym.

JOHN: Oh, yeah. I think Mum wanted to cry but she wasn't going to in front of anyone else. It might be better I leave them alone tonight. To talk and all.

TIM: Slumber party? Mum set up the sunroom—of course.

JOHN: Cool.

TIM: Could sneak back in here later like old times. Bloody sunroom. You're not my girlfriend home from the social. Reckon Mum'd beg Juliet to share a bed with me now. I'm still in grade nine but Anna gets trumpeters and a banquet.

JOHN: What's your gripe with Anna?

TIM: I think I need to tell them.

JOHN: About what?

TIM: About my status.

JOHN: Tim. You can't.

TIM: Why?

JOHN: The wedding. You can't do it the week of Anna's wedding.

TIM: I know that. I know. But it's coming. And how much preparation can I do? I can't read every book and ask every counsellor . I'm just nervous about the wedding; being in front of all those people. And today I read … I read something today …

JOHN: What?

TIM: No, I'm reading that book is all. It's actually called *Telling Your Parents You Have HIV*.

JOHN: I am reeling from Mum and Dad, Tim. Please don't be selfish.

TIM: What?

JOHN: When the time's right. This isn't just a single conversation. This isn't one piece of info. This is telling them everything. They'll want to know everything. What, are you going to paint a picture of your seizure—tell them you were on the floor of the toilet—in a puddle of piss and shit looking over your shoulder and twitching? You going to give them that image to take into your sister's wedding?

TIM: I'm not going to do it the week of the wedding.

JOHN: Or the week that I tell mine.

TIM: My ears are burning. Your parents are at home saying I infected you and—

JOHN: There was no discussion about who infected whom.

TIM: Cell counts can be wrong. I know you don't believe it. I know you blame me.

JOHN: Don't tell me what I know.

TIM: What if there was a way to determine who infected whom? You'd want to know, John.

JOHN: I don't want you to undermine my positive thinking.

TIM: Err, that's from that play.

JOHN: What?

TIM: That Alex Harding play we saw.

JOHN: I liked that play. They didn't believe they were going to die from this.

TIM: Do you?

JOHN: No I don't.

TIM: Is that why we haven't made a will?

JOHN: Maybe we should.

TIM: Only problem is I've got nothing to leave you. You can have my clothes but most of them are yours. It's shit. And anything I treasure was a gift from you anyway.

Enter MARY-GERT.

MARY-GERT: There's the Mercurochrome for your leg.

TIM: Thanks. It's tiny. [*To* JOHN] You do it, John.

MARY-GERT: I'm glad you opened your letters.

TIM: Just leave them. I read them. [*To* JOHN] On my calf. It's dried up anyway.

JOHN *puts the antiseptic ointment on* TIM.

JOHN: I'll draw a smiley face.

MARY-GERT: I put them in your book on your bag.

TIM: I'm reading that for my work.

MARY-GERT: I know … I assumed that.

TIM: I should help you with your platters.

MARY-GERT: Yes. Flat out …

TIM: I like the smoked salmon one best.

MARY-GERT: Yes.

TIM: Could I have lunch with you and Dad tomorrow?

MARY-GERT: We'll all have lunch at some stage.

TIM: No. Just the three of us.

JOHN: Tim.

MARY-GERT: [*calling out to* DICK] Dick.

TIM: No, don't get him.

MARY-GERT: Tell me everything's alright.

JOHN: Tim.

TIM: No it's okay.

Enter DICK.

MARY-GERT: Tim wants to talk about something.

DICK: Oh, what now, Timothy?

TIM: I just want to talk about something.

DICK: Go on then.

TIM: No not now. Tomorrow. We'll have lunch.

DICK: You'll make madam fret. Tell us now, Tim.

TIM: I'll discuss it tomorrow.

DICK: No. Go on. Tell us.

TIM: Well, come sit down.

JOHN: Tim.

TIM: [*to* JOHN] Do you want to stay?

JOHN: [*to* TIM] You grab me if you want me.

JOHN *exits.*

TIM: Come sit, Mum. There's something I've wanted to tell you for some time but didn't think I could. I love you and I'm afraid I'm going to hurt you. John and I have HIV, the virus that can cause AIDS.

MARY-GERT: What a waste. All that talent.

TIM: I'm not dead yet.

DICK: How long have you boys known?

TIM: We were tested five years ago. That's when we were tested.

DICK: And how is your health?

TIM: Mine's pretty good but John's is failing. He's already had pneumonia.

MARY-GERT: That beautiful boy. I knew something was up. He doesn't look well. I said that.

DICK: What does it mean? Do you have AIDS?

TIM: No. I have HIV. I think it would be a good idea … They have counsellors, at the AIDS Council, where I work.

DICK: This is a terrible blow.

MARY-GERT: I knew there was something because you were spending so much money on travel. Italy and then Bali. We didn't even get to see photos of Italy.

TIM: We stopped taking them. I have one: John with this disgusting sore on his face standing in front of Michelangelo's Pieta. He got a fever. We barely saw Florence. We came home early.

MARY-GERT: But I don't understand how you got it. If it's just you and John—

TIM: We both have it.

DICK: Yes.

TIM: John has had to leave his chiropractic clinic.

MARY-GERT: God help us.

TIM: He was too sick to cope with patients' questions. My suppressor cells are at a good stage and my other cells are basically good.

MARY-GERT: We don't know what any of that means.

DICK: I am going to go for a drive. Think I might.

MARY-GERT: Oh. You sure, dear?

DICK: I think I want to. I'll buy the cherries.

MARY-GERT: Okay, dear.

DICK *exits.*

I think you'll be comfortable in here. I put an extra blanket on.

TIM: I think you should see the counsellor. I can arrange it through work.

MARY-GERT: Okay, Tim.

TIM: Dad won't.

MARY-GERT: No. Probably he'll decline.

TIM: That's okay.

MARY-GERT: I should sew this hem. So much to do. Anna's got dinner underway. A difficult week.

TIM: I opened those letters this morning. I read the letters and—

MARY-GERT: Good.

TIM: Mum. The letters were chasing me up … I made a blood donation in June 1981. It was pooled with nineteen others. I'm one of the last to be contacted. The patient who received the blood has developed

AIDS and I might have given it to this poor person. I had a strange viral thing back in '81. I think that may have been my seroconversion.

MARY-GERT: What does this mean?

TIM: I've had it for nine years not five, Mum. So I had to tell you.

MARY-GERT: I see.

TIM: And it means I probably infected John.

MARY-GERT: I see.

TIM: They want a written response. I'll write to the blood bank and tell them everything—that I was tested positive in '85.

MARY-GERT: And that you didn't know. How could you know? Nobody knew then.

TIM: I can't tell John now. I don't want to share this letter with him tonight. I was comfortable with the thought John had infected me, but it's awful to think I may have infected him. As though I've killed the man I love.

[*Aside*] I never wrote the letter to the Red Cross.

Belvoir Street Theatre. ACTORS *sit on mismatched chairs.*

THEATRE DIRECTOR: Is all our company met? Not quite. Ah, Tim! Here he is: the playwright. Excellent.

TIM: Hello.

Hellos.

Sorry I'm late, everyone. I've had this lurgy. I woke up with a fever and could barely get up. Sorry.

THEATRE DIRECTOR: Great. Hope you're better.

TIM: Keep your distance.

THEATRE DIRECTOR: Okay. Now, we had been talking generally about the play and your wonderful changes for our staged reading. Sit there, Tim.

One spare chair is for TIM *but strangely it is a wheelchair.*

TIM: In that?

THEATRE DIRECTOR: Sure. Gia, you said—

ACTOR ONE: Me? Oh just a small thing really, um, about whether the subject matter of your play is right.

TIM: Oh okay.

ACTOR ONE: It's just that maybe the next thing you write, maybe that should be of a world you really know about.

THEATRE DIRECTOR: Yes, okay. And Ben, what did you make of Tim's play?

TIM*'s chair is unstable.*

TIM: Sorry, is my chair rolling?

THEATRE DIRECTOR: You right, Tim?

TIM: Yeah.

ACTOR TWO: It was unclear to me whether you'd moved your bowels today? I couldn't tell really.

TIM: Pardon? My chair's rolling.

ACTOR THREE: Your haemoglobin is still good. Very good.

TIM: [*the wheelchair*] Are there brakes?

THEATRE DIRECTOR: [*the rehearsal*] At eleven. You right?

ACTOR ONE: Your T-cell count reads as three-hundred-and-seventy.

TIM: Why has it changed?

THEATRE DIRECTOR: We wanted to make some cuts.

TIM: Am I late? Where's John?

ACTOR THREE: He's gone, mate. You okay?

ACTOR TWO: Nurse?!

THEATRE DIRECTOR: [*to* ACTOR TWO] Remember to breathe.

TIM: Fuck. John's hurt. He's broken his leg on the top oval playing footy. His mum and dad and Father Wallbridge are at the hospital now turning off the life support machine. Dreamer. I'm too hot. No more warm ups. Excuse me, I'm in the middle of a workshop of a play, my play, I wrote it and tomorrow is the last day's rehearsal yesterday or a decade ago. Or two decades ago. Or three.

ACTOR THREE: You have some leukoplakia on the side of your tongue.

ACTOR ONE: We think it is Epstein-Barr virus, we're having the dramaturg look at it.

ACTOR TWO: When it presents as oral hairy leukoplakia it's considered an AIDS-defining illness.

TIM: Did he say AIDS? Right, it's AIDS everyone, not just HIV, note exposition to heal before opening night with the sleep of the dead, but fuck it's thirty-nine-point-four degrees celsius o'clock and when's Monday? If you feel right by then, I'll be happy for you to go. Oh thank you. Can you stick your hands in your head? Oh no.

ACTOR ONE: The critic who did your bronchoscopy said he saw cysts that are consistent with PCP.

THEATRE DIRECTOR: I think we should start with a fantastic—
ACTOR THREE:—course of Pentamidine.
ACTOR ONE: It's fairly toxic.
THEATRE DIRECTOR: Might be good to get it up on its feet.
ACTOR TWO: How am I meant to piss in this thing? Nurse.

TIM *tries to dress into a jacket and tie.*

TIM: Comb my hair shave suit spew in the sink and one small step dizzy nurse buzz fuck it.
THEATRE DIRECTOR: Will you make it to the reading? Your public awaits.
TIM: [*to* THEATRE DIRECTOR] I don't think I can go. I'm not going in a wheelchair. Knowing my luck I'd vomit in the foyer and, these monsters, under my bed, they'll drink my blood if I step into an operating theatre venue so I can't go I'm afraid. I'm so afraid. I have AIDS. Do people know that, should I make it clearer, for the audience, for my friends, that are here tonight, that'll be there tonight, at the theatre, should I tell them, what should I tell them?
ACTOR ONE: 'Conigrave writes with an exuberant gaze.'
THEATRE DIRECTOR: We'll make up a story ... That you have really bad gastro.
ACTOR THREE: That you're dead and died long ago.
ACTOR TWO: Oh no. Nurse.

An answering machine beeps.

ACTOR ONE: They pissed themselves, Tim. Everyone was devastated you couldn't make it.

An answering machine beeps.

ACTOR TWO: Hi Tim, hope your gastro is getting better. I loved doing your play. Write another one.

An answering machine beeps.

JULIET: [*voiceover*] Tim, it's Juliet. Your play was great, I nearly wet myself. Hope you get a production and that your gastro gets better.

An answering machine beeps.

PETER: [*voiceover*] Peter here, Tim. I told Juliet you were in hospital. I assumed she already knew. Sorry. Call me.

An answering machine beeps.

JULIET: [*voiceover*] Tim, darling, it's Juliet again. You're in hospital? Why didn't you tell us? Is everything okay? Sorry to ask, but everyone is wondering if you have AIDS.

The answering machine beep becomes a life-support machine.

The following three voices overlap.

VOICE: Hi Tim, I've just heard that you are in hospital and that you have AIDS. Is that true? I don't want you and John to die. I'm scared.

VOICE: I've just heard you guys are not well, that you have AIDS. You guys are both the ones I'd least expected to get it. How sick are you?

VOICE: You poor bastards. You poor bastards. Oh god. You poor poor bastards. Oh god.

TIM: I'm fine.

Faint recorded audience laughter.

I'll be back at work in a couple of days.

Recorded audience laughter, growing. TIM *strains to hear where it is coming from.*

But I'm not as weak as you think.

Recorded audience laughter. The Theatre Director has a cassette tape for TIM.

THEATRE DIRECTOR: The cast made a tape of the reading for you. It's hard to hear but I guess you know all the lines.

Recorded audience laughter.

TIM: They're laughing. I made people laugh.

The recording of TIM*'s play fades.*

The Hotel Ramada Renaissance*, Circular Quay.* TIM *and* JOHN *wear jackets and ties.*

Can I have a ciggie?

JOHN: No.

TIM: On the balcony? Please? You can see the Opera House. Let me have a ciggie.

JOHN: No.

TIM: Why?

JOHN: Um, because you've had pneumonia and PCP.

TIM: Oh, who hasn't?

JOHN: You think everything's a joke to be laughed at.

TIM: Shoosh. We're treating ourselves this weekend.

JOHN: You eat McDonald's and Tim Tams behind my back and it stresses me.

TIM: [*as a public announcement*] All kids, please report to the Giggle Palace, all kids.

JOHN: Don't you want to get well?

TIM: Oh Jesus—Fuck, what's up with all the rules?

WAITER: [*offstage*] Room service.

Enter a sexy WAITER.

TIM: Come in if you're beautiful. [*To himself, on seeing the* WAITER] Ooh shit.

WAITER: Good evening.

The WAITER *wheels in their meals.*

TIM: Mr Caleo, will you join me?

JOHN: Thank you.

TIM: Have you worked here long?

WAITER: Two years.

TIM: Must have been at school when you started.

WAITER: Still at school.

TIM: Oh.

TIM: Champagne for Mr Caleo please.

JOHN: Can't.

TIM: Can.

JOHN: Can't. My stomach. I can't.

WAITER: Very good. Will there be anything else, sir?

TIM: Um. No. Oh …

TIM *hands the* WAITER *a tip.*

WAITER: Thank you, sir.

TIM: Bye.

The WAITER *exits.*

JOHN: Did you give him a twenty?

TIM: Yeah.

JOHN: That's too much.

TIM: Well?

JOHN: Well I already felt bad about spending all this money on staying here and you bought a new tie and it worries me.

JOHN *flicks at the meal receipt on the table.*

You are making my ulcer worse.

TIM: We just need some glamour.

TIM *pours* JOHN *some champagne.*

JOHN: My stomach will kill.

Silence.

Sorry. We'll have a nice time tonight.

They start to eat.

Six months is nothing.

TIM: Pardon?

JOHN: It's November.

TIM: I know.

JOHN: I was side-swiped when the doctor said 'lymphoma'. I heard it before he said it.

They eat.

TIM: You could call Peter in Melbourne to help with your decision. He's known you so long … He's a nurse in this field even and he knows what chemo will do and what it means if it is disseminated.

JOHN: I'm calling the doctor on Monday. They said they'll start straight away. I'm taking the ten percent chance of chemo.

TIM: You say it like I should know.

JOHN: I'm not going to give up without a fight.

TIM: A toast. To your decision.

JOHN: To the obvious choice.

TIM: I wish there were others.

They drink.

I spoke to Peter. I called him.

JOHN: You never call Peter.

TIM: He said he could take some leave to help us later in the year.

JOHN: We'll see.

Silence. They eat.

I wish I'd got to play for Essendon.

TIM: Yeah. I wish that too. Will chemo make your eyelashes fall out?

JOHN: I don't know. AZT made them grow longer.

TIM: Really?

JOHN: Think so.

Silence. They eat.

JOHN: I wish I'd been a chiropractor for longer.

TIM: You started your own practice. No regrets there.

JOHN: No. Sure.

TIM: I'm sad my acting career didn't take off.

JOHN: You did alright. I'm sorry I never got to have sex with a woman. There's no way I could now.

TIM: I wanted to have kids with Juliet. Probably a turkey baster but maybe we'd root. Scared I'll get duped on legacy.

JOHN: No-one to look after us when we're old?

TIM: Something like that. So do you really desire to have breeder-sex?

JOHN: I'm curious.

TIM: What if you decided you liked it better than with me?

JOHN: Not a possibility. You're too cute.

Silence. They eat.

TIM: John, there's something I want to tell you. I played around a bit when you were away last year. I'm sorry.

JOHN: I thought with this AIDS stuff that would have stopped.

TIM: I'm sorry.

JOHN: Why do you do this to me? Was it anyone I know?

TIM: Well, no. No.

JOHN: Who?

TIM: Couple of guys in the sauna.

JOHN: I feel like that's not the truth.

TIM: No.

JOHN: It hurts.

Silence. They eat.

TIM: That's my biggest regret. All the times I hurt you.

JOHN: Mmmh. Don't want to talk about that.

TIM: No.

They eat. JOHN *fiddles with the meal receipt, reads it.*

JOHN: They've called us 'Mr and Mrs Conigrave'.

TIM: No? Show me.

JOHN: I'm keeping this receipt.

TIM: [*aside*] He was himself again in an instant. He was himself again as he had been after every other time I'd hurt him.

[*To* JOHN, *a toast*] To my darling John, for the years of love, comfort and support.

JOHN *raises his glass.*

JOHN: Thanks for being my boyfriend.

TIM: Cheers mate. To all the times you let me fall asleep in front of the TV with my head in your lap. All the times we laughed.

JOHN: No wuckers. Thanks for the holidays. Europe and everything. And thank you for being here now.

TIM: It's been fun.

TIM *leans across to kiss* JOHN *but spills his champagne.*

Shit.

JOHN: Such a dag.

They kiss.

St Vincent's Hospital, Sydney. JOHN *sleeps.* TIM *is by his side. Enter* DR SHEPHERD.

DR SHEPHERD: [*to* TIM] Hello, Tim. I just want to ask you some questions.

TIM: What are those tablets?

DR SHEPHERD: How is being in here for you?

TIM: Content. I'm enjoying myself. Except for the hospital smells.

DR SHEPHERD: What sort of things have you been doing to occupy your time?

TIM: I'm writing a play.

DR SHEPHERD: A play? You feel creative?

TIM: Yes. It's called *Jimmy, an Angel, Stars and That* about a gay relationship where one partner is dying. I'm thinking of having a reading with some actor friends one day in the waiting room. You're welcome to come.

DR SHEPHERD: You seem very up, very chatty—

TIM: I just feel good because John won; we've just got good news about John.

DR SHEPHERD: Tim, I'm going to put you on Haloperidol. You're manic because the cells in your brain have become hypersensitive to certain neurotransmitters. Haliperidol reduces the sensitivity. You can take this one now. You've had your breakfast?

TIM: Yes. Do you think I am losing my mind?

DR SHEPHERD: I can't say dementia and memory loss won't happen.

TIM: Will I still be able to write?

DR SHEPHERD: We'll know as your toxo improves.

TIM: Who would have thought: they have unhappy pills too.

DR SHEPHERD: They'll bring them with meals.

TIM: You're going to watch me take it.

DR SHEPHERD: Yes.

TIM *takes the tablet. Enter* BOB CALEO.

TIM: And here's Bob. Well, works quick.

BOB: Hello Doctor, I'm Robert Caleo, John's father. Anything new?

TIM: No Bob, she's my shrink. We got great news. Yuck. [*The pill*] Tastes gross.

DR SHEPHERD: I'll call on you in a week, Tim.

TIM: Bye.

DR SHEPHERD *exits.*

Bob, good news.

BOB: Brought you this from the flat.

BOB *hands over some envelopes.*

TIM: Oh thanks. Bills and stuff, hey?

BOB: [*leaning over* JOHN] Hello John, it's Dad.

TIM: Bob, he's asleep.

BOB: Pardon?

TIM: We got good news. About John.

BOB: Well, I'm all ears.

JOHN: Dad?

BOB: Hello, Son. What have the doctors been saying?

JOHN: Cancer's gone. They just want [*coughs*] keep trying to fix my lungs by [*coughs*] antibiotics in them.

BOB: What … ?

JOHN: Cancer's gone.

BOB: … I'm sorry, I can't hear him.

TIM: [*to* BOB] He can't speak loudly; it makes him cough. John's doctor was here. The scope showed that the ulcer's gone. He's pretty sure. John beat it.

BOB: Ulcer? The Cancer?

TIM: John's cancer is in remission.

JOHN: Haven't you got [*coughs*] hearing aid?

BOB: What did he … ?

TIM: Asked if you've got your hearing aid.

BOB: [*to* TIM] I don't like wearing it. [*To* JOHN] The cancer, you've worked hard for it, son.

TIM: Here, Bob, have my seat.

JOHN: [*coughs*] All the cards will stop.

TIM: [*to* JOHN] Don't strain yourself, John.

[*To* BOB] He said the cards will stop.

BOB: He's hardly one hundred percent.

JOHN: I only [*coughs*] cards for cancer.

TIM: Says he only gets cards for cancer.

BOB: Well, John, your mother prefers that, telling people that you have cancer.

JOHN: But it was AIDS-related cancer.

TIM: Don't strain. I can do it.

BOB: It's something for you to take up with her.

BOB *pulls out another envelope with notes scrawled across it.*

Now, listen, mate, I was reading your will this morning.

JOHN: Where [*coughs*] you get that from?

BOB: Pardon?

TIM: John wants to know where you got his will from.

BOB: [*to* JOHN] It was in the drawer of your desk. I have some concerns. Why is everything going to Tim?

JOHN: Shit. [*coughs*] want to make sure he's alright if I die.

BOB: I didn't get any of that.

TIM: He said he wants to make sure I'm alright if he dies.

BOB: And Tim, is your will set out similarly?

TIM: It is.

BOB: And if John doesn't survive you?

TIM: It goes to my family.

BOB: So if John dies, you inherit his belongings. And then say a month later you die? Everything goes to your family? I don't think that's fair. I would like half. I put John through school and college and I think I deserve it. I made a list this morning. Now, who owns the television and video?

TIM: They're John's.

BOB: What about the car? You don't want it, Tim, do you? With all the stuff going on in your brain?

TIM: They're resolving, Bob. But I'm not going to fight you for it. You can have it.

BOB: And the bed?

TIM: Well there are things we bought together. Can I have a look?

BOB *hands* TIM *the list.*

BOB: All right.

TIM: Yeah, it might be better for John and me to go through the list for you, Bob.

BOB: All right.

TIM: [*reading the list*] Because it looks pretty thorough. CDs and videos. Just trying to think who bought the Vegemite last. Probably you, John.

JOHN: [*to* TIM] It hurts my lungs to laugh.

TIM: [*to* JOHN] Sorry.

BOB: Well, you go through it then.

TIM: [*quietly to* JOHN] And the boy videos; your family would enjoy 'Frisky Pool Party 7'.

BOB: That's right.

JOHN: [*to* TIM] Stop it.

BOB: Might grab some breakfast then.

TIM: And some little red dots to mark up the apartment.

JOHN *sniggers.*

BOB: Goodo.

JOHN *coughs.*

TIM: [*to* JOHN] Sorry.

BOB: Some things are only fair.

BOB *exits.*

TIM: There's still hair from arsehole to breakfast.

JOHN: The chemo's stopping. I don't have cancer.

TIM: It's ratty. Will you let me clipper it?

TIM *lifts off* JOHN*'s wig to reveal a shaved head. As* JOHN *exits—*

PETER: Good to be home?

And now we're at ***Tim and John's apartment****.* PETER *is dressed for tennis. He collects his racquet.*

TIM: Where'd you come from?

PETER: You look tired.

TIM: Peter?

PETER: Yes.

TIM: You're in my home. I can manage.

PETER: You're tired.

TIM: And don't tell me I'm tired, Peter.

PETER: Okay. You're snapping and irrational because of the toxo and—

TIM: Get real.

PETER: Well you may not want my help—

TIM: Fuck off.

PETER: But I know John does. And I'd do anything he asked.

TIM: It's not a three-way relationship, Peter.

PETER: Just here to help, Tim.

TIM: Peter, he's been sleeping with his eyes half open.

PETER: That's okay. It's normal.

TIM: His cough keeps me up and last night I dreamt he got bitten in the stomach by the devil. I don't want us to go mad, Peter. I don't want you to say that about us. It's not true.

PETER: I know.

TIM: Where would his soul go—trapped inside his madness or floating free?

PETER: Ask a priest. I'm a nurse. Try to get some sleep, Tim.

TIM: Did he vomit again?

PETER: I had to reinsert his tube. Tim, work is prepared to give me leave so I can be John's carer.

TIM: I'm his carer.

PETER: A professional carer. It's what I do.

TIM: So if I get like John, if I get like John without John, will you do this for me?

PETER: Tim … John and I, we never really fit in with all the theatre people and the uni crowd. We were on the sideline and that was good.

TIM: I never slept with Woody.

PETER: Woody? I know.

TIM: You slept with John a few times.

PETER: 1980 was a long time ago.

TIM: Not long enough. Time moves too fast.

PETER: I nursed Lee.

TIM: Lee?

PETER: Lee from university. He was mates with Woody.

TIM: Lee? Lee gave me a swampwater milkshake at my first Gaysoc meeting.

PETER: I barely recognised him—only when I looked at the name on his file. I went to his funeral. He didn't last long. I can't escape it. Every patient's a friend or a lover of a friend or … John's talking about going up north. If you need me to stay and to travel, call me.

TIM: Thank you for doing the laundry and stocking the fridge and everything. We laughed because—did you even buy condoms?

PETER: Can't remember them on the list.

TIM: We made love last night. Maybe for the last time.

PETER: It's going to happen.

TIM: He wanted to be fucked, for me to fuck him.

PETER: You don't have to tell me everything, Tim.

TIM: When he came there wasn't much fluid and that's probably a sign of how sick he is. We hadn't had anal sex since, way back, John said, 'That's how we got into this mess in the first place.' Last night, he seduced me and undressed me and I felt just how skinny he's got; rolling around, caught up in his tubes. It almost didn't work and I said we didn't have to but he wanted me to fuck him and we persisted and he took me inside him. Then we lay there and he slept and slept. That was such a gift, giving of himself. If John wants to go on a trip to somewhere warm, we should let him.

PETER: We'll organise it. Byron maybe. I'll sell my Sleaze Ball tickets and come with you.

TIM: He fights too hard.

PETER: He cries for you daily, Tim. He's afraid you'll face death alone. I'm going to be late. Dinner's in the fridge.

PETER *exits.*

Enter JOHN. *He has tubes twisted and trailing.*

TIM: John? Did you wake up?

JOHN: We have to get the cricket whites. The other team will be here in a minute.

TIM: John, what are you talking about?

JOHN: The Australian cricket team. They're coming on the supply ship.

TIM: Where are we?

JOHN: Christmas Island.

TIM: Oh okay. But John, we're in Sydney. In our apartment.

JOHN: What about the team?

TIM: It's alright, Johnny. I think we should go to see the doctor.

JOHN: I'm not sick. We went to Coffs Harbour.

TIM: Yeah. We're back. We went on our holiday with Peter. To Byron Bay. I have to go see the doctor and I'd like you to come with me.

JOHN: And we're going to Melbourne for Christmas.

TIM: We'll talk to the doctor about that.

JOHN: We're going home for Christmas.

TIM: Okay, sweetie.

TIM *manoeuvres* JOHN *back to bed.*

Fairfield Hospital*, Melbourne.* TIM *hums 'Jingle Bells' as he reveals* JOHN*'s present.*

TIM: It's a stable-table.

JOHN: [*grinning*] There's something for you under the bed.

TIM *retrieves his present and removes the black and red wrapping paper.*

I got Peter to get it for me.

TIM: Oh, darling, what on earth is it?

JOHN: It's a document holder for writing. It's got a little motorised clamp that moves up and down when you use the foot pedal.

TIM: It's bizarre.

JOHN: You don't like it.

TIM: It's good, but I don't know if the clamp is all that useful. [*Aside*] You always have to tell the truth, don't you, Timothy?

JOHN: For when you write.

TIM: I should.

JOHN: It's wrapped in Essendon colours.

TIM: Always. I like it. I'll use it. I promise. Your first present to me was wrapped in Essendon colours. You wrote on the card, 'No longer sweet sixteen, hope the next seventeen are as much fun. I love you. John.'

JOHN: You remember that?

TIM: Maybe I'm paraphrasing but I don't think so. And the present was Bryan Ferry's 'Let's Stick Together'.

JOHN: That's right.

TIM: You told me that you'd seen him on 'Countdown' and he'd made you feel a bit sweaty.

JOHN: Did I?

TIM: And I remember then you looked around and checked the coast was clear and you snuck in a kiss on the lips. I remember that. And then the bell went and we went to Geography together. Maybe it isn't attacking my brain anymore.

JOHN: Nup. Your brain's too big.

TIM: You've always outdone me on presents, John.

JOHN: Yesterday didn't hurt a bit. I was just not here and now my ribs are all bruised from the bloody cardiac massage. I wish I'd gone. It was so easy, Timba. Are you okay hearing that?

TIM: No, I'm not ready for you to go.

JOHN: We've said our goodbyes, haven't we?

The ACTOR PLAYING JOHN *stands and retrieves a puppet of his withered self. This puppet will take* JOHN*'s place for the remainder of the play.*

TIM: You can't go without me at your side.

JOHN: I know.

TIM: That's the deal.

JOHN: I love you, Tim.

TIM: I love you too.

TIM *kisses the puppet. The* ACTOR PLAYING JOHN *remains on stage.* JOHN*'s breathing underscores the scene.*

Enter LOIS. *She reaches into her bag and pulls out two salad rolls.*

LOIS: Just salad. I hope that's okay.
TIM: Thank you. There's that fold-out: you're welcome to sleep on it.
LOIS: Might sit up for a bit. Thank you.
TIM: You've got the time?
LOIS: About one a.m. You probably haven't slept much.
TIM: No. Feeling it. Juliet and Peter have been great.

TIM *rubs the puppet and* JOHN*'s groaning softens.*

LOIS: Bob and I found a nice grave this morning. Yesterday. It's under a tree, and we're having a boulder as a headstone with a brass plaque on it. Do you like the sound of that?
TIM: I think that's good.
LOIS: And Bob and I are going to be buried with him. We'd like that.

Silence but for JOHN*'s breathing.*

You have a sleep if you like.
TIM: Weird: tomorrow's Australia Day.
LOIS: January flies.
TIM: Especially when you're—My sleep's so shallow. Did I sleep then?

If they did sleep, we did not see it. Time is slipping.

LOIS: Think I did. It's near three.

JOHN*'s breathing underscores.*

TIM: Don't think I did.
LOIS: John, will you shut up, we're trying to sleep.

They laugh.

He is such a gentle soul. This is what I was afraid of. He loved you, Tim.
TIM: I hope he knows how loved he is, how many phone calls I get: people who say how unfair it is and how he's the nicest person they've ever known.

LOIS: He was my favourite. I shouldn't say it, all my boys are wonderful. But he was my favourite. Never a problem.

TIM: Bob spoke to me about the car, Lois. I said I didn't want it but—

LOIS: You don't have to deal with Bob. You come to me. The car is yours.

JOHN's groans become louder. Enter BOB, PETER *and* JULIET. *They surround the puppet.*

TIM: [*aside*] Blind fear—schoolboy about to get the strap. Bob and Lois holding your hands—Peter and Juliet at your feet. Where am I supposed to sit?

TIM *slides in behind* BOB *and strokes* JOHN*'s head.* BOB *pushes in front of* TIM *and kisses* JOHN*'s forehead.* JOHN*'s breathing is soon shallower, quieter and then a new noise and a different exhale.* BOB *grabs a tissue and wipes the puppet's chin.*

They wait. JOHN*'s breathing stops.* JOHN *is dead. Silence.*

After a moment BOB *wanders around the room putting things into a plastic bag. Only the* ACTOR PLAYING JOHN *is watching as* TIM *lowers his hand onto the puppet for their final touch. Exit* LOIS *and* JULIET.

BOB: *The Melbourne Age*, January 27, 1992.

PETER: *The Sydney Star Observer*, January 30, 1992.

BOB: Caleo, John Robert.

PETER: John Caleo.

BOB: Sleep peacefully my son, now there's no more pain.

PETER: We won't forget your fighting spirit and your kind and innocent heart.

BOB: You will always be remembered until we meet again.

PETER: Our love and support to Tim Conigrave, John's partner in life for the past fifteen years.

BOB: All our love, Mum, Dad, Michael, Paul, Christopher and Anthony.

Exit BOB *and* PETER.

TIM: Dear John,

I am sitting in the garden at the back of my hotel, surrounded by orange trees and bougainvilleas. After the madness of the northern cities, the island of Lipari is paradise.

I visited the island of Salina yesterday, the island where your grandparents were born. It was a bit like a private pilgrimage. It is almost barren, lots of rock and caper bushes. The café is only open for an hour and you can understand why they emigrated.

The most unnerving thing: here on Lipari there is a beautiful boy who works in the bar in our hotel. He is so like you he could easily be one of your brothers. He was born here but his family is not Caleo. He is so gentle and so shy. We try to talk but he speaks Liparota, a dialect I can't understand. He occupies my dreams. I fall in love so easily these days.

Life is pretty good at the moment: I have my health and seem to be doing most of the things I want to do before I die. I guess the hardest thing is having so much love for you and it somehow not being returned. I develop crushes all the time but that is just misdirected need for you. You are a hole in my life, a black hole. Anything I place there cannot be returned. I miss you terribly.

The ACTOR PLAYING JOHN *leaves the stage.*

Ci vedremo lassù, angelo.

ACTOR PLAYING TIM: Timothy Conigrave died in October 1994, ten days after he completed his memoir *Holding the Man*, a gift to John. The end.

THE END